THE DAY AND THE HOUR

THE DAY AND THE HOUR

Is sooner than we think

Robin Hitsman

TATE PUBLISHING & Enterprises

Published by Tate Publishing & Enterprises, LLC
127 E. Trade Center Terrace | Mustang, Oklahoma 73064 USA
1.888.361.9473 | www.tatepublishing.com

Tate Publishing is committed to excellence in the publishing industry. The company reflects the philosophy established by the founders, based on Psalm 68:11,
"The Lord gave the word and great was the company of those who published it."

Book design copyright © 2011 by Tate Publishing, LLC. All rights reserved.
Cover design by Blake Brasor
Interior design by Lindsay B. Behrens
Illustration by Joshua R. Hitsman

Published in the United States of America

ISBN: 978-1-61777-046-3
Religion / Christian Theology / Eschatology
11.01.31

DEDICATION

This book is dedicated to all those who desire with all their heart to receive their glorified spiritual bodies, who hate sin and love righteousness. You are precious to the LORD.

Acknowledgments

I acknowledge each person who has been appointed by our heavenly Father to teach his people, through the Word of God, to be watching and to be ready to meet the LORD in the clouds when we hear the trumpet blow.

TABLE OF CONTENTS

INTRODUCTION

You can likely tell by the title *The Day and the Hour* that this is another book on the coming of the LORD. There have been so many books written on this very important topic that most Christians do not even give this topic a second thought anymore. They have resigned their mind to think that when he comes, he will come. Materials written on the coming of the LORD in these times are now only considered to be nothing more than speculation.

Unfortunately, with this kind of attitude, many Christians can actually close their ears to what the LORD is speaking to them. Do you know that the LORD expects everyone who belongs to him to be watching and to be ready for his coming? He actually commands it! But if we Christians are not interested in his coming, then how can we obey what he says? Do you also know that our salvation is not complete until Jesus comes for his church? This is not my opinion, but it is what the Bible teaches. This is the Father's plan for his new creation (the church).

If you have just come into a relationship with your Savior, then I implore you to not let anyone tell you that we do not need knowledge on this topic. I know there will be those who will teach you that we cannot know when he will come. These people are only the blind leading the blind. The Word of God clearly reveals the generation of the second coming of the LORD Jesus Christ, and the catching away of the body of Christ is even before that. Jesus's own words pinpoint his coming to redeem the nation of Israel with absolute accuracy. All we have to do is understand what it is that he is speaking.

You may have noticed an unfamiliar phrase in the previous paragraph—*catching away*. This phrase is more commonly known as the rapture of the church. I have decided to use this phrase rather than the word *rapture* to appease those who stand firm that the term *rapture* cannot be found in the English Bible. I will not go into the explanation of this either, because it has been overexplained, and there are still those who argue this point. But we do read in our English Bibles that the church is *caught up,* as it says: "Then we who are alive, who are left, will be caught up together with them in the clouds, to meet the LORD in the air. So we will be with the LORD forever" (1 Thessalonians 4:17, HNV). So I do not put any hindrance in the minds of any interested reader; I will use the phrase *caught up* instead of *rapture.* But this is the only appeasement you will get out of me, so hang on to it.

The second coming is something every Christian needs to pay attention to. Although we will not be here to go up in it, we will be coming down in it. The Father's plan is for us to be caught up from this earth supernaturally at least seven biblical years before the second coming. The second coming is actually for the remnant of Israel and not for the new creation. But we, who are the new creation, or the church of Christ, use the second coming as a gauge so we can keep our eye on the day of the catching away. The material I present in this book will further explain what I mean by this statement and will help every reader to gauge with more accuracy these two very important events.

I have written the material in this book so that each chapter builds on each other to show with clarity how close we are to experiencing the day of the catching away. We who belong to the LORD are expected to know this information, as I will prove from God's own Word.

This book is written to all those who have put their faith in the LORD, Jesus Christ, and have received God's salvation. This book is written to induce each one to get serious in their relationship with the one who is most holy. Some might say that they do not need any book but the Bible to teach them about their relationship with the LORD and that this is just another book. I will not disagree with you; but the compilation of material in this book will allow God himself to teach you, with his own Word, about your relationship with him. I just encourage each one to let the Holy Spirit teach you; so listen to what he has to say. The Holy Spirit is the only one who can help each of us to ensure Jesus stays as our first love. I pray the Holy Spirit will guide each one who reads this book and will reveal God's truth with exceptional clarity.

Why Parables?

Jesus often used parables to communicate his message about the kingdom to his people. He would teach in parabolic language to communicate the message of the kingdom to all who would come to hear what he had to say. And many wanted to hear what Jesus was teaching, for the words he spoke were like no one else could speak. The other teachers of religion and philosophy were not able to compare to this new Jewish rabbi. The people in the LORD's hometown of Nazareth were astonished at the wisdom that came from him, for it says this about Jesus: "Coming into his own country, he taught them in their synagogue, so that they were astonished, and said, "Where did this man get this wisdom, and these mighty works?" (Matthew 13:54)

The people were surprised at Jesus's words of wisdom and the mighty works of miracles that were coming through him, because they had a supernatural element to them, which the people had never heard or seen before. But even more than this, Jesus was one of them. Jesus was one of the hometown boys, who worked with his (earthly) father, Joseph, and, likely, his younger brothers in the carpentry trade. His fellow Jews saw Jesus grow up from a little boy to manhood, and without a doubt, most of these people grew up alongside him. The people in the synagogue would have known the family of Joseph all their lives; this is why they made this comment:

> Isn't this the carpenter's son? Isn't his mother called Miryam (Mary), and his brothers, Ya`akov (James), Yosi (Joseph), Shim`on (Simon), and Yehudah (Judas)? Aren't all of his sisters with us? Where then did this man get all of these things?
>
> Matthew 13:55–56

The people of Nazareth were outraged at Jesus with jealousy because of the capacity of his wisdom and the mighty power of God coming from him. Jealousy can cause people to think all kinds of strange and wicked things. These Nazarenes probably thought in this vein: *Why does this carpenter's son have all this ability and not one of us? How come one of the sons from one of the more prominent families in the community are not blessed with this supernatural power instead of the one who just works with wood?* Of course, these thoughts are only conjecture on my part. Jesus's contemporaries should have been amazed at the mighty power of God working through him, instead of being offended by him, and recognized that a prophet of God was in their midst. This is why Jesus responded to them when they were offended with this remark: "A prophet is not without honor, except in his own country, and in his own house" (Matthew 13:57).

KEEP THEM CONFUSED

Jesus would use parabolic language quite frequently when speaking to the crowds, and he would do it for a couple of reasons: First, to make it difficult for those who were trying to incriminate him, as an enemy of Rome, with the things he was teaching. It says this in the Gospel of Luke:

> Woe to you lawyers! For you took away the key of knowledge. You didn't enter in yourselves, and those who were entering in, you hindered." As he said these things to them, the Sofrim (Scribes) and the Perushim (Pharisees) began to be terribly angry, and to draw many things out of him; lying in wait for him, and seeking to catch him in something he might say, that they might accuse him.
>
> Luke 11:52–54

The scribes and the Pharisees were always trying to entrap Jesus in his words, so the LORD would speak in parables, and they could not comprehend the message(s) he was teaching. The priests and the scribes were very crafty in their attempts to catch Jesus with something they could use against him, as it says this in Luke:

> The chief Kohanim (Priests) and the Sofrim (Scribes) sought to lay hands on him that very hour, but they feared the people—for they knew he had spoken this parable against them. They watched him, and sent out spies, who pretended to be righteous, that they might trap him in something he said, so as to deliver him up to the power and authority of the governor.
>
> Luke 20:19–20

Jesus would speak in parables so they could not pinpoint any one idea he was teaching and use it against him. As said, the teachers of the law were extremely jealous of Jesus, to the extent that they would attempt to take the things Jesus was teaching and twist it so they might deliver him up to the Roman officials with charges of inciting an insurrection. This method of teaching with symbolic language made the scribes and the Pharisees furious with Jesus, because they were unable to trap him in his words.

REVEALING THE MYSTERIES

Another reason why Jesus taught with parables, the primary reason, was to reveal the mysteries of the kingdom of heaven. We read this in the Gospel of Matthew:

> The talmidim (disciples) came, and said to him, "Why do you speak to them in parables?" He answered them, "To you it is given to know the mysteries of the kingdom of heaven, but it is not given to them.
>
> Matthew 13:10–11

The mysteries of the kingdom of heaven are for the *people* of the kingdom and not for those who are outside of it. Initially, Jesus was referring to the disciples when he said, "The mysteries of the kingdom have been given to you," but the disciples are the foundation of the household of God, with Jesus being the chief cornerstone, and we are being built on the foundation. The apostle Paul wrote this in the letter to the Ephesians:

> So then you are no longer strangers and foreigners, but you are fellow citizens with the holy ones, and of the household of God, being built on the foundation of the apostles and prophets, Messiah (Christ) Yeshua (Jesus) himself being the chief cornerstone; in whom the whole building, fitted

together, grows into a holy temple in the LORD; in whom you also are built together for a habitation of God in the Spirit.

Ephesians 2:19–22

So the good news is, the mysteries of God are for *you* and *me* too.

The word Matthew used that we translate *mysteries* refers to things that are secret or things that are hidden from natural comprehension. Jesus primarily taught using parables, because he was teaching the secrets of the kingdom of God, and these things which are hidden are only for those who are of the kingdom. Anyone who receives Jesus Christ as LORD by grace through faith becomes a citizen of this kingdom. The "kingdom of heaven" and the "kingdom of God" mean the same thing. The two phrases are interchangeable. They both refer to the spiritual realm of God and all aspects of it.

THE FARMER WHO SOWS SEED

There are many examples we could use to see how Jesus taught using parabolic language, but I thought we would use the parable of the farmer who went out to sow seed. This is a good example, because this parable also reveals the varying results when the Word of God is planted into a person's heart.

In the parable of the farmer who went out to sow seed, we see in Matthew 13:4–8 that when seed is planted, four things can happen:

1. Birds can come and devour what seed is planted if it is not planted properly, for instance, if it falls carelessly on the roadside.

2. The seed can be scorched by the sun and wither away if it is planted where the seed can't take root, like on rocky places.

3. If the seed is planted where there are thorns, the thorns will choke the seed.

4. If seed is planted on good soil, it will grow and produce a harvest.

JESUS EXPLAINS

After Jesus taught this parable to the crowds, he then went on to explain his teaching to the disciples in Matthew 13:18–23, where he led off by saying this: "Hear, then, the parable of the farmer" (Matthew 13:18). If a person does not understand the word of the kingdom when he hears it, the devil will come and steal what was planted in them. As Jesus explains, "When anyone hears the word of the kingdom, and doesn't understand it, the evil one comes, and snatches away that which has been sown in his heart. This is what was sown by the roadside" (Matthew 13:19, HNV). Now typically this teaching is used to explain why the unbeliever does not receive Christ, which is that they do not receive the Word first. Without receiving the Word, one cannot have faith to believe in the Savior, because faith only comes from the Word. But this first illustration, of seed being sown by the roadside along with the following three, would also refer to the believer who does not grow in the faith. For example: Some Christians, after they receive the gospel message and receive Jesus as Savior, are not able to receive much more of the Word of God because they choose not to. They are content with the seed they received initially at salvation because they believe they have "made it" as many pastors would agree with this. This group of Christians are only limited to the milk of the Word, and skim milk at that, because they are not able to handle any solid food. When the Word is preached and taught at a deeper level, which is the meat of the Word, this group cannot understand it, so the enemy comes and steals it from their heart. Thus, this group of milk-only Christians have the seed sown in their life week after week, but because they cannot understand what they hear, the devil robs them of it.

Jesus continues and explains that when one hears and receives the Word, they can endure for a while, but because the person's heart is too hard for the seed to take root, they quickly begin to stumble or be offended because of tribulation and persecution. The Greek word used that translates "to stumble" refers to being lead into sin and also to fall away from faith. This is what Jesus says:

> What was sown on the rocky places, this is he who hears the word, and immediately with joy receives it; yet he has no root in himself, but endures for a while. When oppression or persecution arises because of the word, immediately he stumbles.
>
> Matthew 13:20–21

These people are Christians who have received the Word and received it with joy because their understanding has been enlightened to their salvation. But because the seed cannot take firm root, these people are led back into sin, and some even fall away from the faith. This happens because they cannot hold onto the Word that saved them when oppression and persecution arises because of the Word. They cannot hold on because the Word has not taken root. Understand what has been said: The seed has been planted in their heart, and they endure for a while, but because they do not break up the hard ground (their heart), the seed cannot produce fruit properly. This is not referring to the Word being planted in the mind, because Jesus makes it clear in verse nineteen that the Word is being planted in the people's hearts.

Next, there is the person who receives the Word, but because of the cares of this world and the anxiety it brings, along with the love of money, the Word does not grow. This person's spirit is likened to a thorn bush as it says, "What was sown among the thorns, this is he who hears the word, but the cares of this world and the deceitfulness of riches choke the word, and he becomes unfruitful" (Matthew 13:22). Do not let the version of this verse that I am using deceive you into thinking this group did not receive the Word. This translation (which is a good one) just assumes the reader understands that this group receives the Word just like the other groups did. The translation of the Bible you may use most likely says this group receives the Word also. The Word cannot grow in these people primarily because they are unable to understand the Word beyond the stages of infancy, like the first group; therefore, they are in danger of falling away like the second group.

INTERPRET WHAT IS BEING REVEALED

As I have already mentioned, anyone can take these three groups and categorize them within a group who has never received salvation. But we must interpret this passage with the message that is being revealed. One cannot have the Word sown (received) into their heart without a transformation taking place. It is when a person does not receive the Word when they hear it that the transforming power of the Word cannot even begin. It says this in 1 Corinthians: "Now the natural man doesn't receive the things of God's Spirit, for they are foolishness to him, and he can't know them, because they are spiritually discerned" (1Corinthians 2:14). The Word of God comes from God's Spirit. In fact, the Spirit breathes the Word of God. If the Spirit does not breathe a word, it is not the Word of God. It is impossible for a person to receive the Word of God and remain a natural man. The reason why the natural man is not transformed into a new creation is because the Word of God, which is spiritually discerned, is foolishness to him or her, so they do not receive it into their heart. These people in Jesus's teaching received the Word of God when it was sown into them. Because they received the seed sown, they received the "things of God's Spirit" (1Corinthians 2:14a); thus, they were transformed and then able to discern the spiritual.

GOOD GROUND

Lastly, there is no debating whether this fourth group was of the Spirit. These people received the Word into their spirit, and because their spirit is good ground, they have the potential to understand the deeper things of the Word. It says in Matthew:

> What was sown on the good ground, this is he who hears the word, and understands it, which most assuredly bears fruit, and brings forth, some one hundred times as much, some sixty, and some thirty.
>
> Matthew 13:23

The Word will bear much fruit in these people, implying much understanding or insight into the mysteries of the kingdom of heaven. It is this group about whom Jesus said, "He who has ears to hear, let him hear" (Matthew 13:9). "Let him hear" means to hear and understand what Christ is teaching. Only those with a heart made of good ground will have the ears to hear what the Bible is really teaching, especially the mysteries of the kingdom.

Jesus had to explain this parable to the disciples when they were away from the crowds. These people could not understand Christ's teaching because they did not have ears to hear and understand. Jesus knew there was no need for him to teach the crowd of people other than the disciples the meaning of his parable, because he knew they still would not understand. Jesus spoke of these people, saying, "Therefore I speak to them in parables, because seeing they don't see, and hearing, they don't hear, neither do they understand" (Matthew 13:13). The mysteries of the kingdom of heaven are for the people of the kingdom and not those who are outside of it. The Holy Spirit is able to teach the body of Christ the hidden mysteries of the kingdom. The Christian has also to be good ground to be fruitful so he or she can produce a crop of understanding. Bearing fruit producing one hundred, sixty, and thirty times what was planted.

How blessed are the people who hear and understand the mysteries of the kingdom of heaven, as it says: "But blessed are your eyes, for they see; and your ears, for they hear" (Matthew 13:16). At the time Jesus taught this parable, he was teaching his people Israel, but not all of them had the ability to understand what he was really teaching. Only those whose hearts were good ground were able to hear and understand the mysteries of heaven. And then their understanding was made clearer after they were actually took aside and taught by the teacher. Jesus generally spoke to Israel in parables to fulfill Scripture (see Psalms 78:2), as it says in Matthew:

Yeshua (Jesus) spoke all these things in parables to the multitudes; and without a parable, he didn't speak to them, that it might be fulfilled which was spoken through the prophet, saying, "I will open my mouth in parables; I will utter things hidden from the foundation of the world.

Matthew 13:34–35

GETTING GOOD GROUND

We get the right kind of ground by cultivating our heart. We cultivate our heart by studying, mediating, obeying, and speaking the Word of God. The evidence of good ground will be faith in the person of God and completely believing what he says in his Word. The apostle Paul writes this in Romans: "So faith comes by hearing, and hearing by the Word of God" (Romans 10:17). Hearing the Word of God cultivates and makes our spirit ground good. As Christians, we must not block our ears to truth we don't want to hear. We need to hear and understand every truth that God is speaking to us through his Word. We must get out of the habit of just picking and choosing what it is we want to hear from the Word of God. Many Christians produce very little understanding of the Word of God because there are portions of the Word where they will not go. The reason may be because of conviction, but mainly it's because their pastors and teachers do not take them there. Because most Christians put their trust in their leaders, they tend not to know enough to go any place in the Word of God where their pastors do not lead them.

Another example of getting good ground is praying in the unknown language, which comes by being baptized in the Holy Spirit. And I must add, praying in this power everyday at length. If you are not baptized in the Holy Spirit with the evidence of speaking in an unknown language, as we see in Acts 2:4, then might I suggest you seek God on this issue with seriousness? Praying in an unknown language is not a denominational doctrine, although some of the church thinks it is. But it is not; it is the Word of God. This book is not devoted to teach on the power of the Spirit, which is God's will for all those who belong to him. But there are many good books which teach on this subject. Might I again suggest to you to check them out? The Bible tells us how to pray, which will cultivate our heart and make it good ground, as it says in Ephesians and Romans:

> With all prayer and requests, praying at all times in the Spirit, and being watchful to this end in all perseverance and requests for all the holy ones.
>
> Ephesians 6:18

> In the same way, the Spirit also helps our weaknesses, for we don't know how to pray as we ought. But the Spirit himself makes intercession for us with groaning which can't be uttered.
>
> Romans 8:26

PRESSURE HELPS TO CULTIVATE

The Holy Spirit will put pressure on the believer to be good ground. We need to stop resisting the Spirit of God and open ourselves up to the mysteries of the kingdom of heaven. The mysteries are in the Word, so will we hear and understand them? Sadly, many believers find the urging and leading the Holy Spirit uses as being too much, likely because they only want to hear familiar portions of truth and nothing else. This is like taking only part of Jesus instead of all of him. Many Christians also do not live by faith in the Word of God but by their five senses only. They do this because they are not yet good, cultivated ground. They are like the seed that is planted on rocky ground, and the Word cannot take root within them. When more seed is being planted, they let it fall by the roadside because they are content only with the Word that was planted in them to receive salvation. The gospel message that leads us to salvation is only the first step. Unfortunately, many do not go beyond that point. Because some do not want to receive from God beyond their initial step, they sadly begin to fall back. When oppressions and persecutions come, they begin to go back into the sin that once entangled them. The Word cannot produce in some other people because: "The cares of this world and the deceitfulness of riches choke the word" (Matthew 13:22).

I exhort my brothers and sisters: let us turn it around. Jesus said the knowledge of the mysteries of the kingdom have been given to those whom he has chosen. That means you and me! At least the disciples were on the right track when they demanded of Jesus this request in Luke: "The apostles said to the LORD, 'Increase our faith'" (Luke 17:5). Do you notice the apostles did not ask the LORD but *told* him to increase their faith? The Greek word used to translate the word *said* also can be translated as *tell*, which has the connotation to command or give an order. The LORD does not mind us being forthright in our faith. He wants us first and foremost to believe and not doubt the things he says.

KNOW THE MYSTERIES

Jesus parables were more often than not prophetic. It requires deep insight into the Scriptures to understand what Jesus is prophesying through his teachings. Those who are of the kingdom will, through a sincere devotion to study and an ear to heaven, gain understanding to the mysteries of the kingdom. The mysteries are not hidden to us like they are to those who are not of the faith. We just have to dig into the Scriptures with the help of Holy Spirit and anointed teachers to understand these hidden things. In this book the Spirit will reveal to you some important mysteries for this generation. The hidden things are revealed to us with just a little devoted studying. Most of the hidden things have been brought to the surface already with time, but many Christians do not know it. They know more about what is on television than they do about the Word of God. I have been guilty of this same thing, but I heeded the call and turned it around. If you are a son or daughter of the kingdom, then the mysteries of the kingdom are for you.

If we are to be ready for the day and the hour when the Son of Man will appear, then we need to desire the Word of God more than ever before. We will see in this book some of the mysteries of the kingdom pertaining to the catching away. We could only know them in this generation because of the unfolding revelation that has occurred. We need to be watching and ready because the *day and the hour* of the LORD's coming for his bride is *sooner than we think.*

THE FIG TREE

As we discussed in chapter one, Jesus's normal method of teaching was to speak using parabolic language. At the sake of repeating what we have already discussed, Jesus did this because the mysteries of the kingdom of heaven have been given to the household of God, not to the people who stand by their own will, let alone outside of it. The household of God refers specifically to those whose lives are built upon the foundation of the apostles and prophets, with the LORD Jesus Christ being the chief cornerstone. It is only those who sincerely believe in the name of Jesus who can understand what Jesus is saying in his parables. And then the household generally needs help with the interpretation, as did the disciples.

THE ANOINTING HELPS
Today's church needs anointed teachers who have actually received the ministry office of teacher to teach them what the Word is saying, especially the deeper things hidden in God's Word. Yes, there are many teachers who are not directed by the spirit of God and who teach only their own opinions, which have no foundation in the Word of God whatsoever. We see this written in 2 Peter:

But there also arose false prophets among the people, as among you also there will be false teachers, who will secretly bring in destructive heresies, denying even the Master who bought them, bringing on themselves swift destruction.

2 Peter 2:1

But if the Christian is sincere in his or her relationship with the Father, they will have ears to hear what the Spirit of God is saying. The Spirit of God will improve the ability of their spirit to discern who the false prophets and false teachers are. Likewise, they will have supernatural ability to discern if the prophet and teacher speak by the Spirit of God.

UNDERSTANDING THE FIG TREE

To help us to understand the day and the hour of the LORD's glorious appearing, meaning his coming for the body of Christ, we need to understand the parables of the fig tree, because they give us good insight into this event. They give us good insight into the season of the catching away, because the teachings on the fig tree in the Gospels help reveal the second coming of Christ. When we get the revelation into the second coming of Christ and its approximate timing, then we have revelation into the catching away of the body of Christ.

So let us look at the fig tree to see its significance to the second coming of Christ for the Nation of Israel. But before we discuss the fig tree in the Gospel accounts, we need to see how the fig tree relates to Israel in the old covenant, where the fig and the fig tree are mentioned quite often. Here, the Jewish people are also represented by the fig fruit, either by the fig fruit itself or the fig tree.

Understanding the Fig: Old Covenant

We read in Jeremiah chapter twenty-four:

> The LORD shown me, and, behold, two baskets of figs set before the temple of the LORD, after that Nevukhadretztzar [Nebuchadrezzar] king of Bavel [Babylon] had carried away captive Yekhonyah [Jeconiah] the son of Yehoiakim, [Jehoiakim] king of Yehudah, [Judah] and the princes of Yehudah, [Judah] with the craftsmen and smiths, from Yerushalayim, [Jerusalem] and had brought them to Bavel [Babylon].
>
> Jeremiah 24:1

In Jeremiah 24:2–3, we see that one basket has very good figs and the other basket has very bad figs. The two baskets of figs represent the southern portion of Israel's kingdom.

We see in Jeremiah 24:5 that the captives of Judah, who were sent out of Jerusalem into Babylon, are symbolic of the very good figs. We see also in this passage that the very bad figs are symbolic of those whose hearts were hardened, as it says in verse eight: "Tzidkiyahu [Zedekiah] the king of Yehudah [Judah], and his princes, and the residue of Yerushalayim [Jerusalem], who remain in this land, and those who dwell in the land of Mitzrayim [Egypt]" (Jeremiah 24:8). The reason why the LORD considered this latter group as symbolic to very bad figs is because Zedekiah did not humble himself to the prophet Jeremiah when the prophet came speaking to him with the Word of the LORD. Instead, Zedekiah became stiff-necked, which refers to being stubbornly proud, and turned his heart away from the LORD. The people mentioned along with Zedekiah, the princes and the residue of Jerusalem, "trespassed very greatly after all the abominations of the nations; and they polluted the house of the Lord" (2 Chronicles 36:14b).

The prophets also used the fig tree to refer to Israel and her position with God in Jeremiah 8:13; 29:17; Hosea 2:12; 9:10; Joel 1:7, 12; Micah 7:1; Habakkuk 3:12; Haggai 2:19 and Zechariah 3:10. So as we see, the Lord uses the fig fruit and its tree many times to represent the nation of Israel. Of course, God not only uses the fig and its tree to represent Israel in Scripture, but it is one object he uses frequently. He also used a prostitute in the book of Hosea to illustrate Israel's relationship with him (see Hosea 1:2).

THE FIG LEAF COVERING

It is no wonder the God of Israel would use the fig and its tree to represent his people so often, considering the fig is a very familiar fruit in the Middle East. We know the fig fruit was one of the first foods man cultivated because after Adam sinned against the Lord and ate of the tree of the knowledge of good and evil, Eve and he sewed leaves from the fig tree together to cover up their nakedness. It says this in Genesis chapter three: "Both of their eyes were opened, and they knew that they were naked. They sewed fig leaves together, and made themselves aprons" (Genesis 3:7).

There is a symbolic message between the fig fruit and its tree and the fig leaves used by Adam and Eve to cover up their nakedness after breaking covenant with the Lord their God. God purposely refers to Israel as the fig fruit and its tree as a reminder to Israel of the covenant that the first Adam broke between him and God. The fig fruit and its tree symbolically represent unfaithfulness to the covenant of God. God made a covenant with Adam that he and his offspring would be the gods of this earth (now do not let this phrase disturb you), with complete dominion over the earth and everything God created in it (see Genesis 1:28–30). But Adam broke this covenant by eating from the tree that God told him not to, and Adam attempts to cover up his transgression with a fig leaf.

MADE IN GOD'S IMAGE

Do not let the idea that God made man to be the gods of this earth confuse you or shut down your ability to reason. I did not say that God made man to be God. But God did make Adam to be like him. It says in Genesis chapter one: "God created man in his own image. In God's image he created him; male and female he created them" (Genesis 1:27). So God made man in his own image, which means God made man a self-willed, speaking spirit just like God. God then gives this self-willed, speaking spirit a body made of flesh, created from the earth to live in. To strengthen my remark, I suggest you read one of the Psalms of Asaph, as he writes this: "I said, 'You are gods, All of you are sons of Ha`Elyon [the Most High]'" (Psalms 82:6). So here it says that the sons of the Most High God are gods, which has the meaning they are the gods, or rulers, of God's creation. Then we read this in Psalms chapter eight:

> What is man that you think of him, the son of man that you care for him? For you have made him a little lower than God, and crowned him with glory and honor. You make him ruler over the works of your hands. You have put all things under his feet: All sheep and oxen, Yes, and the animals of the field, the birds of the sky, the fish of the sea, and whatever passes through the paths of the seas.
>
> Psalms 8:4–8

Some will say that this passage refers to Jesus. But if we carefully study Hebrews 2:5–9, we can see that this passage refers to the first Adam and the second Adam (Jesus) both.

When we make reference to God making Adam and Eve the gods of this earth, it means that they were made more than just natural human beings. God crowned them with glory and honor, which represents his divine supernatural ability was in them and rested on them like a crown. Adam originally had God's ability, before he fell, to speak and create just like God, because Adam had God-like faith. Jesus said this in Mark chapter eleven:

> For most assuredly I tell you, whoever may tell this mountain, 'Be taken up and cast into the sea,' and doesn't doubt in his heart, but believes that what he says is happening; he shall have whatever he says. Therefore I tell you, all things whatever you pray and ask for, believe that you receive them, and you shall have them.
>
> Mark 11:23–24

The ability Jesus describes in these two verses takes God like faith to achieve. Adam had this ability created in him by God but then lost it when he broke covenant with God. It is not wrong to say Adam and Eve were created to be the gods of this earth; they were just not to worship themselves or each other but only their Creator.

ADAM'S ACTION
We come back now to the covenant that God made with Adam, and we see the only thing that would break the covenant is if Adam ate from the tree in the middle of the garden, which was

the tree of the knowledge of good and evil. God said this to Adam in Genesis chapter two:

> The LORD God took the man, and put him into the garden of Eden to dress it and to keep it. The LORD God commanded the man, saying, "Of every tree of the garden you may freely eat: but of the tree of the knowledge of good and evil, you shall not eat of it: for in the day that you eat of it you will surely die.
>
> Genesis 2:15–16

"The day that Adam should eat of the tree he would surely die" refers to not only spiritual and physical death for Adam and his descendants but also that God's covenant with Adam to have dominion over all his works on the earth would be broken. In fact, Adam's actions broke the covenant, and as a result, Adam unknowingly handed his dominion over to Satan. Satan outwitted Adam.

This covenant was broken through Adam's disobedience to God's Word not to eat of the tree in the middle of the garden. The covenant was temporally put on hold until God would send the second and last Adam, meaning Jesus Christ, to legally take Adam's dominion back from Satan. Jesus, in turn, outwitted Satan when he took back man's dominion, as it says in the first letter to the Corinthians:

> But we speak God's wisdom in a mystery, the wisdom that has been hidden, which God foreordained before the worlds to our glory, which none of the rulers of this world has known: For had they known it, they wouldn't have crucified the LORD of glory.
>
> 1 Corinthians 2:7–8

If Satan would have known that Christ's death on the cross would result in him losing man's dominion over the earth, he would have never inspired the people to crucify him. The leaves from the fig tree that Adam used to cover himself were an instrument Adam used to indicate that he sinned against God by eating from the tree of knowledge of good and evil, which broke the covenant of God with him. Keeping in mind this broken relationship between God and Adam, with Adam being the initiator and the fig leaf being the indicator, we see in the writings of the prophets and the gospels that God uses the fig fruit and its tree to represent the nation of Israel, who continually broke covenant with him.

ISRAEL'S COVENANT (BROKEN)

God's covenant with Israel can be found in Exodus chapter nineteen, which says:

> Now therefore, if you will indeed obey my voice, and keep my covenant, then you shall be my own possession from among all peoples; for all the eretz [earth] is mine; and you shall be to me a kingdom of Kohanim [Priests], and a holy nation.' These are the words which you shall speak to the children of Yisra'el [Israel].
>
> Exodus19:5–6

This covenant is known as the *mosaic covenant,* since Moses was God's chosen leader over Israel and God gave it to the people through him. When we read the history of Israel, we see that they also broke covenant with God through their continual disobedience to his voice. We read this in Jeremiah chapter thirty-one:

Not according to the covenant that I made with their fathers in the day that I took them by the hand to bring them out of the land of Mitzrayim [Egypt]; which my covenant they broke, although I was a husband to them, says the LORD.

Jeremiah 31:32
(Also see Jeremiah 11:8–10; 22:9.)

This covenant is also temporally suspended until the second coming of Christ Jesus, when he will come and redeem Israel from her disobedience, in which they will finally live under this covenant as "a kingdom of priests and a holy nation" (Exodus 19:6a).

So can we now see the correlation between the fig leaf, which served as the indicator, or the symbol, of the broken covenant between God and Adam? And can we also see why Israel was symbolically referred to as a fig and its tree by God? It is because Israel continually broke the covenant God made with her at Mount Sinai. We see the fig fruit and its tree were used as a symbol representing Israel's unfaithfulness to the covenant of God.

NO NEED FOR SUPERSTITION

This does not mean that the fig and its tree have some curse associated with it or that we should never eat the fig fruit again because it is was used to represent unfaithfulness to God. But we can surely notice all throughout Scripture, God speaks in various ways to communicate to his people. As the prophets spoke the Word of God to Israel and used the fig fruit and its tree to refer to them, they were using symbolic language to make reference to Israel's continued unfaithfulness to God's covenant. When Jesus used the fig tree to symbolically represent Israel in the Gospels, he was also speaking to them as a prophet because they were still unfaithful to God's covenant.

THE FIG TREE: IN THE GOSPELS

Now that we have a little clearer understanding of the fig and its tree in the old covenant, we will now look at it in the Gospels. The fig tree passages help us to understand Israel's spiritual condition in the days when Jesus was ministering on the earth; plus, as previously mentioned, they help us to know the season of the second coming of Israel's Messiah. And knowing the season of the second coming gives the church of Jesus Christ greater insight into knowing the approximate time of the catching up of his people.

Twice in the Gospels Jesus uses the fig tree in parables. The first one is found in Luke 13:6–9, which is the parable of the man who had a fig tree planted in his vineyard. We will look at this one right away. The second parable of the fig tree is found in Matthew 24:32; Mark 13:28; and Luke 21:29–30. We will not look at this second parable until chapter four. Then there is a third teaching with the fig tree as the center of attention. Jesus has an actual encounter with this fig tree in which he speaks a curse over it, whereby it withers up and dies. This is found in Matthew 21:18–19 and Mark 11:12–14, 20–21. We will look at the symbolic message behind this incident in chapter three of my book. The nation of Israel is represented by the fig tree in all three of these Gospel passages.

THE MAN AND HIS FIG TREE

In the Gospel of Luke it reads:

> A certain man had a fig tree planted in his vineyard, and he came seeking fruit on it, and found none. He said to the vinedresser, "Behold, these three years I have come looking for fruit on this fig tree, and found none. Cut it down. Why does it waste the soil?" He answered, "LORD, leave it alone this year also, until I dig around it, and fertilize it. If it bears fruit, fine; but if not, after that, you can cut it down."
>
> Luke 13:6–9

Before we discuss the context of this parable, we will first take a look at the symbolism within it:

A. The word *fig* symbolically represents the Jewish people whom God has purposely labeled them with this symbol because of their continued unfaithfulness to him.

B. The word *tree:* This term is typically used in Scripture to symbolize a nation. As an example, you can read Ezekiel 31: 3–18.

C. Therefore the term *fig tree,* in the context of this parable, represents the nation of Israel.

D. The *man who had a fig tree* planted in his vineyard is God. He owns both the fig tree and the vineyard.

E. The *vineyard* symbolically represents Jerusalem and the land of Israel.

F. The *vinedresser* is the angel of the LORD.

Some interpreters have thought this vinedresser symbolically represents Jesus. But it is better to equate Jesus with the man (God) who owns both the fig tree and the vineyard. It is the angel of the LORD who carries out the spoken Word or the command of God to perform Gods work in and through the spiritual realm, and the results are made manifest in the physical realm. In this parable, the angel of the LORD (the vinedresser) is the one who receives the command of the LORD (the man who owns the vineyard). The angel in this parable carries out the work of the LORD attempting to get the fig tree (Israel) to produce fruit.

The following are some examples of the work of the angel of the LORD:

A. God sent an angel to Yerushalayim [Jerusalem] to destroy it: and as he was about to destroy, the LORD saw, and he repented him of the evil, and said to the destroying angel, it is enough; now stay your hand. The angel of the LORD was standing by the threshing floor of Ornan the Yevusi [Jebusite]. David lifted up his eyes, and saw the angel of the LORD standing between eretz [the earth] and the sky, having a drawn sword in his hand stretched out over Yerushalayim [Jerusalem]. Then David and the Zakenim [elders], clothed in sackcloth, fell on their faces.

1 Chronicles 21:15–16
(Also in 2 Samuel 24:16–17)

B. It happened that night, which the angel of the LORD went forth, and struck in the camp of the Ashshur [Assyrians] one hundred eighty-five thousand: and when men arose early in the morning, behold, these were all dead bodies.

2 Kings 19:35

C. The angel of the LORD encamps round about those who fear him, and delivers them.

Psalms 34:7

D. For he [God], will give his angels charge over you, to guard you in all your ways.

Psalms 91:11

(I added both examples C and D to deliver you from any anxiety you may have experienced from examples A and B.)

Remember Jesus said that he spoke in parables because the *mysteries* or the *hidden things* of the kingdom of heaven were only for those who are of his kingdom and not for those who are outside of it. "He [Jesus] answered them, "To you it is given to know the mysteries of the kingdom of heaven, but it is not given to them" (Matthew 13:11). The people who stand outside of God's kingdom cannot see, hear, or comprehend, what Jesus is teaching: "Therefore I speak to them in parables, because seeing they don't see, and hearing, they don't hear, neither do they understand" (Matthew 13:13). Therefore, in this parable of the man who had a fig tree planted in his vineyard; we need to have eyes to see, ears to hear, and a heart that understands what the LORD is saying.

ISRAEL'S PURPOSE: TO BEAR FRUIT

The nation of Israel was planted to bear spiritual fruit for God. She was supposed to be a testimony of the grace and power of God to the nations of the earth or, symbolically speaking, to the other trees of the earth. The lack of fruit from this fig tree in this parable symbolizes no spiritual fruit being produced by the nation of Israel.

In ancient times, a fruitful fig tree grown on the soil of any nation was known to be a symbol for prosperity and blessing for that particular nation. Oppositely, the barren fig tree was a symbol to represent that nation was cursed. This adage is not something declared from heaven but was a saying believed in the hearts of natural men.

JESUS GIVES AN EXAMPLE

When we look at the verses that precede this parable in Luke 13:1–5, we see that Jesus was comparing the spiritual condition of the Galileans, who suffered and died at the hands of Pilate, with the other Galileans who did not suffer such tragedy. We read this in Luke chapter thirteen: "Yeshua [Jesus] answered them, "Do you think that these Galileans were worse sinners than all the other Galileans, because they suffered such things?" (Luke13:2). He compares their spiritual condition by using the phrase: "Were [they] worse sinners then all the other Galileans" (Luke 13:2a).

Then from the same passage, in Luke 13:1–5, Jesus compares also the spiritual condition of the eighteen men who lived in Jerusalem, who were killed when the tower of Siloam fell on them, with all the other men who were residing in the holy city. It says this in verse four: "Or those eighteen, on whom the tower in Shiloach [Siloam] fell, and killed them; do you think that they were worse offenders than all the men who dwell in Yerusha-layim [Jerusalem]?" (Luke 13:4). Jesus compares the spiritual condition of these men also when he said, "Do you think that they were worse offenders than all the [other] men [of Jerusalem]?" (Luke 13:4b).

To help us to understand what Jesus is saying in his symbolic teaching of the man who had a fig tree planted in his vineyard, we need to consider what Jesus just finished saying in Luke 13:1–5 and the two examples he gave. Let us look at two key statements Jesus made pertaining to the destiny of these men who died tragically. Jesus gives this stern warning: "I tell you, no, but, unless you repent, you will all perish in the same way" (Luke 13:3, 5). So what Jesus was saying was if Israel did not repent, they would all perish like these other men. Jesus was not referring to physical death but spiritual death. The Greek word used for *perish* means in the broadest terms to be destroyed completely, which refers to body, soul, and spirit.

Jesus was able to use the passage from Luke 13:1–5 as a lead in to his parable of the fig tree that was planted. He is speaking about Israel's history and prophetically about their future through this parable. Some have taken this parable and tried to make it refer to the church of Christ, but in doing this, we make Jesus's teaching refer to a group of people whom he did not intend it to have reference to. The church is never referred to as fig fruit or a fig tree in Scripture. This parable, along with the other two Gospel references pertaining to the fig tree, and the old covenant references given are in reference to the nation of Israel only, which is a separate entity altogether from the church of Christ.

What Jesus Is Saying

Let's take a look at what Jesus is saying to the people in this parable. Jesus says in Luke chapter thirteen, "A certain man had a fig tree planted in his vineyard, and he came seeking fruit on it, and found none" (Luke 13:6). Symbolically, Jesus is referring to the nation of Israel belonging to God. The man (God) had a fig tree (Israel) planted in his vineyard (Jerusalem and the land of Israel). Genesis 12:1–9 says God called Abram, the son of Terah, out of his home country of Haran, and God would make Abram a great nation. God told Abram to go to a land he would show him, which was the land of Canaan. Abram left Haran and settled in Canaan, which later became known as Israel. God promised Abram, whom later he named Abraham, that he would give this land to him and his seed. The seed God was referring to was Abraham's son, Isaac, who was born by supernatural means, and Abraham's grandson Jacob, who later became *Israel,* and the sons of Jacob and their descendants.

Then Jesus says in his parable that the man (God) came seeking fruit on his fig tree (Israel), but none was to be found. Jesus was referring symbolically to spiritual fruit by using a physical fruit analogy. God chose Abraham and his descendants and planted them in Canaan to produce spiritual fruit for him. Just like God expects spiritual fruit to manifest through the new creation (the church), Israel was to manifest the fruit of God to all the nations, or the other "trees" around her, so much so, that the other nations would have the opportunity to see then desire and receive the fruit Israel was suppose to manifest. But as Jesus said, "The man found none" (Luke 13:6c). In verse seven, the man said to the vinedresser, "Behold, these three years I have come looking for fruit on this fig tree, and found none" (Luke 13:7).

What was Jesus referring to by the phrase, "These three years"? (Luke 13:7a). It has to do with Israel's unfaithfulness to God.

GOD HAS BEEN (VERY) PATIENT

As is recorded in the old covenant, we see years of consistent unfaithfulness to God by Israel, but there are three times God dealt with it.

He Came Looking: Once

The first time God dealt with Israel was in 722 BC: The northern kingdom of Israel was captured by King Shalmaneser of Assyria. 2 Kings 17:5–6 says that King Shalmaneser came up through all the northern kingdom and onto Samaria its capital and besieged it for three years (725–722 BC). Finally overtaking Samaria, King Shalmaneser and his armies carried Israel away into Assyria. Why did this happen to the descendants of Abraham the sons of Jacob? We see the reason in 2 Kings 17:7–18: the northern kingdom of Israel was unfaithful to the LORD their God:

> For [so] it was, that the children of Israel had sinned against the LORD their God, who had brought them out of the land of Egypt, from under the hand of Pharaoh king of Egypt, and had feared other gods, And walked in the statutes of the heathen, whom the LORD cast out from before the children of Israel, and of the kings of Israel which they had made.
>
> 2 Kings 17:7–8 (Webster's Bible)

Read for yourself in 2 Kings 17:7–18 all the detestable things Israel did to their LORD. It all adds up to being unfaithful to the covenant God made with them. We see in 2 Kings 17:13–14 God sent the prophets, calling Israel to turn from their evil and keep God's commandments, but they would not listen. God came looking for spiritual fruit on his fig tree, but he found none.

He Came Looking: Twice

The second time God dealt with Israel was in 605 BC. The southern kingdom of Israel was captured by Nebuchadnezzar, the king of Babylon. 2 Kings 24:1–2 says that Nebuchadnezzar, the king of Babylon, came up to Judah and made the king of Judah his servant for three years. The year 605 BC was the beginning of Israel's exile to Babylon with Daniel being part of this first group deported to Babylon (see Daniel 1:1–2). There were two more deportations after this one with the second and third being in 597 and 586 BC. The south was exiled just like the north because of her unfaithfulness to God and his covenant. This was the second time God came looking for spiritual fruit on his fig tree but found none.

He Came Looking: Three Times

The third time God came looking for spiritual fruit on his fig tree was when Jesus came and presented himself to Israel as their king. Luke 19:36–44 tells us the record of Palm Sunday when Jesus rode into Jerusalem on a donkey colt to present himself to Israel as their king. The multitude of disciples were rejoicing, praising God, and making the declaration that Jesus is their king. The Pharisees, on the other hand, did not accept this and told Jesus to quiet down his disciples. Jesus, with tears in his eyes, said to the Pharisees and those who did not believe that they have missed this day. This was the day of God's visitation to them, and they missed it. Israel did not know that this was their day of visitation by the one who was prophesied of in Daniel 9:25. This verse prophesies that Israel's Messiah would come to them on this day, which, when calculated, was April 06, AD 32 (This calculation is explained in the chapter *Daniel's Vision.*) This third time God came looking for spiritual fruit on his fig tree but found none.

God Finds None: But He Is Patient

We can see that three times God came looking for spiritual fruit in his chosen nation, but all three times he found none. In Jesus's parable, the man tells the vinedresser to cut the tree down because it grows no fruit, but the vinedresser suggests the tree be left alone for one more year, and he will dig around it and fertilize it. If the tree does not produce after this, then he will cut it down. Symbolically, this parable is revealing that God will give Israel another chance to bear fruit for him. This will take place during the tribulation period, which is Israel's seventieth week, as prophesied by the angel Gabriel to Daniel (see Daniel 9:24–27). Take a look at this prophesy, and you will see that at the end of the seventieth week, Israel will be finished with disobedience. She will finally receive her Messiah and anoint him her king. In chapter five we will study this vision of Daniel to show that the day and the hour of the coming of the Son of Man is sooner than we think.

The Fig Tree: Without Fruit

Now that we have a clearer understanding of Jesus's parable of the man who had a fig tree planted, let us look at an encounter Jesus had with an actual living fig tree. Just like the parable in the Gospel of Luke 13:6–9, this fig tree also did not produce any fruit and it, too, represents the nation of Israel. We find this story in both the Gospels of Matthew and Mark, which I suggest you read from both records because Matthew records his version of the incident a little different than Mark does. Of course, Mark was only writing what the apostle Peter was dictating to him. But just because the two records have a slight difference in the way they are presented, it does not mean the incident is fabricated in the least, as you are about to read. The differences in the two accounts are not proof, as some have suggested, that the Bible contradicts itself.

Here are the recorded incidences of this fig tree by both Matthew and Mark:

A.   Now in the morning, as he returned to the city, he was hungry. Seeing a fig tree by the road, he came to it, and found nothing on it but leaves. He said to it, "Let there be no fruit from you forever!" Immediately the fig tree withered away. When the talmidim [disciples] saw it, they marveled, saying, "How did the fig tree immediately wither away?

Matthew 21:18–20

B.   The next day, when they had come out from Beit-Anyah,
      [Bethany] he was hungry. Seeing a fig tree afar off having
      leaves, he came to see if perhaps he might find anything
      on it. When he came to it, he found nothing but leaves,
      for it was not the season for figs. Yeshua [Jesus] told it,
      "May no one ever eat fruit from you again!" and his talmi-
      dim [disciples] heard it. As they passed by in the morn-
      ing, they saw the fig tree withered away from the roots.
      Rock, [Peter] remembering, said to him, "Rabbi, look!
      The fig tree which you cursed has withered away.

                                            Mark 11:12–14, 20–21

JESUS ENTERS THE CITY

This story happened in the same week as the crucifixion, beginning on the first day of the week, which was Palm Sunday. Jesus
and his disciples were on the road to Jerusalem, with Jesus on
the back of a young donkey. As they entered the Holy City,
great multitudes started to lay down their garments before Jesus,
while others were cutting off palm branches and laying them on
the road before him. We read this in the Gospel of John:

> They took the branches of the palm trees, and went out to
> meet him, and cried out, "Hoshia`na [hosanna]! Blessed is
> he who comes in the name of the LORD, the King of Yisra'el
> [Israel]!"

                                                  John 12:13

When Jesus and his disciples arrived into the city, they went
directly to the temple. Mark records Jesus looking around at
everything in the temple, but because it was late on the Sunday,

he and the disciples go back to Bethany on the Mountain of Olives, and then they return the next day, which was Monday. If you are at all curious, Bethany is the present-day West Bank town called El-Aziriyeh.

Matthew does not record Jesus leaving the temple or the city on Sunday, as his contemporary Mark does, but instead he writes that Jesus enters the temple and physically throws out those who were buying and selling in the temple. Jesus proceeds to turn the tables of the moneychangers upside down and also the chairs of all who sold doves (see Matthew 21:12). So it seems Matthew is saying Jesus drove these people out on Sunday, but Mark records Jesus throwing these swindlers out of the temple on Monday. It looks like the two Gospel writers did not compare notes with each other, which those who love to criticize the Bible have a great time with. But the difference in their records does not disprove the credibility of this story. In fact, all it proves is the different personalities of the two individuals.

Different Personalities

First, Matthew was a tax collector who we would refer to professionally as an accountant. Accountants are financially minded and, being so, generally think and record everything systematically. So naturally, Matthew the *taxman* would record his account of the ministry of Jesus systematically. It is like when an accountant gathers up the month's end receipts for the fuel used for a fleet of vehicles. He then proceeds to enter all these receipts into an itemized column named *Fuel.* The accountant totals up all the fuel receipts for that given month and enters them into the one column, even though the transactions occurred on different days. This is how a *taxman* would record a specific teaching even though the teaching might be spread out over a lengthy period of time.

Secondly, we see Mark, who is known as John Mark in Acts 12:12. He writes his gospel chronologically because this is what he heard Peter preach. It was from Peter's preaching that Mark compiled his information for his gospel. Mark wrote his gospel in chronological order, meaning he recorded one event after another as they happened, which reveals a more detailed account of when each event truly transpired. Matthew was not concerned about the order of events or when they occurred, only that they happened.

As an example, we can look at Matthew's record of the Sermon on the Mount in chapters five to seven of his gospel. We see that he records it systematically, as would be the natural way a financially minded individual would make a record of a story. But in the other gospels we see this same teaching was taught in intervals, with other events happening in-between. If we notice in the Gospel of Mark, likewise in the Gospel of Luke, the Sermon on the Mount is sequenced throughout their gospels. Bits and pieces of this sermon are injected throughout their gospels because this is how each event truly transpired. Matthew takes this sermon and records it systematically, as he likely believed this would cut down on any confusion by his readers (I hypothesize). But Mark and Luke record the Sermon on the Mount in the order that each portion of it was actually preached, with other events occurring in between, which is chronologically correct.

This is why Matthew does not record Jesus leaving both the temple and Jerusalem the same day as Mark does, because he is only interested in recording all the events surrounding the temple in systematical order. Where Mark records the events surrounding the temple in the order as they happen, which means Jesus arrives at the temple, leaves it, and then comes back the next day. Recording the events surrounding the temple, either systematically or chronologically, does not contradict the truth of the actual events that occurred within the temple. It only has a bearing on the detail of the said events.

It is the same with the day the two recorded accounts say the fig tree withered. Matthew says the fig tree withered immediately, which seems to imply the same day it was cursed. Mark's account seems to imply the fig tree withered the day after Jesus spoke against it. But if we read the language carefully, we see that in Matthew's account, the disciples did not comment about the withered tree until they saw it, which can refer to the next day as Mark records it. But here again the systematic thinker makes the record of this event all in one column, making it seem as though nothing else happened in-between. In all likelihood, the tree fully withered by the next day, as Mark records the chronologic order of the death of this tree.

Both Matthew and Mark show Jesus encountering the barren fig tree on Monday the day after Palm Sunday. But before we can understand why Jesus spoke against this fig tree, we must understand more clearly the temple incident first, because both of these stories have to do with Israel's spiritual condition at that time.

THE TEMPLE RUCKUS

The temple incident was a statement of Jesus's rejection of Israel's spiritual leaders and its religious system. They had turned the temple worship into an event where it was a place to make money. It says this in Matthew:

Yeshua [Jesus] entered into the temple of God, and drove out all of those who sold and bought in the temple, and overthrew the money-changers' tables and the seats of those who sold the doves. He said to them, "It is written, 'My house shall be called a house of prayer,' but you have made it a den of robbers!

Matthew 21:12–13

When we look in the Old Testament at the writings of the prophet Malachi, we see how the temple priests were dishonoring and showing the LORD disrespect. In Malachi, chapter one, it is recorded that the temple priests were offering polluted bread on the altar of the LORD. They were also offering blind, sick, and lame animals to the LORD as well, which the LORD called "evil." We can be almost sure that the animals for sacrifice being sold in the temple when Jesus entered into it were with blemish, as was forbidden. They would have been lame, sick, and blind, as the ones we read of in the first chapter of Malachi. These animals were meant to be without blemish, as a holy sacrifice unto the LORD. However, the spiritual leaders were evil; they did not care about the LORD and therefore just offered him whatever was convenient for them.

The temple was the place where the people were commanded to bring their sacrificial offerings out of obedience to honor God. But Israel's spiritual leaders turned the temple area into a marketplace, where they would sell sacrificial offerings that were defective. Not only that, but they were likely selling them at exorbitant prices for Jesus to call them robbers. Jesus's actions in cleansing the temple area was a symbolic sign that God was finished with what Israel's spiritual leaders had turned their worship into. Their worship practices had become corrupt and insulted him. The temple area, with all this corruption taking place, was a manifestation of Israel's spiritual condition.

Jesus Notices the Fig Tree

Now we can look at Jesus's encounter with the fruitless fig tree and gain a little more insight as to why Jesus would curse it. In Mark 11:12, we see Jesus was hungry after leaving Bethany, and he sees this fig tree having leaves, and he goes to see if there is any fruit on it. In Mark chapter eleven, we read: "Seeing a fig tree afar off having leaves, he came to see if perhaps he might find anything on it. When he came to it, he found nothing but leaves, for it was not the season for figs" (Mark 11:13). Jesus finds no fruit on this fig tree because, as we have read, it was not the season for figs.

Did Jesus not know it was not the season for figs? Why would Jesus curse a fig tree because it did not have fruit, especially if it was not even the season for figs? First of all, as a rule, the fruit of the fig tree appears before the leaves, and the fig is actually considered to be the flower of the tree. The fruit on the fig tree is green until it ripens, so the color of the fruit and leaves blend together until the fig matures, and then its color changes to purple. This incident took place in the month of Abib, which is late March early April, so this is why Jesus, seeing at a distance, assumed there was fruit on the tree, even though it was too early in the season for the fig tree to bear fruit.

Secondly, remember this barren fig tree symbolically represents the nation of Israel. Jesus cursed this fig tree to symbolically represent God rejecting Israel's consistent lack of bearing spiritual fruit, which represents a consistent rejection of his voice. Just as God rejected Israel's corrupt practices in the temple, the cursing of this fig tree represents his rejection of their being spiritual dead. This is the primary reason why Jesus cursed this deceitful fruit tree, which is a symbolic truth. Jesus also used this opportunity to teach his disciples how to pray. If you will notice, in both Gospel accounts Jesus does not use this incident to reveal to them how to pray until after they inquired of him: "When the talmidim [disciples] saw it, they marveled, saying, "How did the fig tree immediately wither away?" (Matthew 21:20).

No Fruit, No Faith

The leaves on this tree represent a religious Israel, but the lack of fruit represents a lack of faith in their God. This fruitless fig tree represents a spiritually dead Israel; this is why Jesus said to it, "No one will ever eat fruit from it ever again" (Mark 11:14). This tree had no fruit, only leaves, like Israel who only had religion, but no spiritual fruit. No wonder the temple worship was in the condition it was; Israel was religious but had no faith in the Lord, their God. The apostle Paul said in the letter to the Roman congregation:

> But Yisra'el [Israel], following after a law of righteousness, didn't arrive at the law of righteousness. Why? Because they didn't seek it by faith, but as it were by works of the law.
>
> Romans 9:31–32

Jesus had to drive out of the temple all who were buying and selling there and overturn the tables of the moneychangers, because they were making the place of worship corrupt. Likewise, he cursed the fruitless fig tree to symbolize his having enough of Israel being religious only and having no faith.

No Fruit, No Faith: But Still Patient

As we see from chapter two, the parable of the man who had a fig tree planted in Luke 13:6–9, Israel will have another chance to bear fruit during the fast-approaching tribulation period known as Israel's seventieth week. When we do a study of Romans 11:1–5, we find that God is not finished with Israel yet. The apostle Paul said God has not rejected his chosen people; in fact, God has reserved for himself in accordance with the election of grace, a remnant.

It would be a benefit to everyone to read and study Romans chapter nine through eleven before you go to the next chapter of this book. You will see from your study how important Israel is in the plan of God.

The Fig Tree Teaches
a Parable

Now that we have looked at two of the three examples, which symbolically speak of the fig tree representing the nation of Israel, let us now look at the third example. We read this from Matthew chapter twenty-four, which says:

> Now from the fig tree learn this parable. When its branch has now become tender, and puts forth its leaves, you know that the summer is near. Even so you also, when you see all these things, know that it is near, even at the doors. Most assuredly I tell you, this generation will not pass away, until all these things are accomplished.
>
> Matthew 24:32–34

The fig tree in this passage represents the nation of Israel, just as it did in the parable of the man who planted a fig tree in the Gospel of Luke and in the passage where Jesus cursed the fruitless fig tree in both the Gospels of Matthew and Mark. Some people *in this generation* do not believe that the fig tree mentioned in Matthew 24:32 and the parallel accounts in Mark and Luke symbolically represent Israel. I have my own opinion for their lack of insight, but I will not share it with you here.

Some of you also have your own opinion of why they cannot see this truth, but it is likely more beneficial for them if we join together and believe their hearts will open to receive this truth. We who have received this knowledge must remember that it says this in 1 Corinthians: "Knowledge puffs up, but love builds up" (1Corinthians 8:1).

Our Church Fathers Knew

The early church knew this parable was a symbolical reference to the nation of Israel, and they were obviously closer to the time when this parable was first being discussed than we are. For example, there is an Ethiopic text of the Apocalypse of Peter, which declares that Matthew 24:32 and Mark 13:28, along with Luke 21:29–30, all represent the house of Israel as the said fig tree.[1] The Apocalypse of Peter is a non-canonical early Christian writing, which dates back to the early part of the second century. It is said by some that the apostle Peter himself is the writer, but I don't know how he could be when he was crucified before the destruction of Jerusalem in AD 70. If Simon Peter was the true writer of this document or if he was not, the writing still circulated among the early Christian church nonetheless. There are various websites that have published *The Apocalypse of Peter* if you are interested in viewing this information. Just make sure you glean the Ethiopic version, as the Greek version does not carry this information.

Israel Will Produce Fruit

We see Jesus say, "Now from the fig tree learn this parable" (Matthew 24:32a). This phrase actually interprets like this: "From the 'fig tree' (the nation of Israel) 'learn this parable' (know the message Jesus is teaching)." What parable or message is Jesus referring to? The parable he is referring to is the phrase that immediately follows, which is, "When its branch has now become tender, and puts forth its leaves, you know that the summer is near" (Matthew 24:32bc). This phrase refers to the fig tree and it beginning to blossom. Through the symbol of this fig tree, Jesus is revealing that Israel will begin to produce spiritual fruit. Jesus is prophesying Israel's restoration as a sovereign nation through this parable.

Remember the parable of the man who planted a fig tree in his vineyard in Luke 13:6–9? This parable symbolically referred to Israel being given opportunity to bear spiritual fruit, but she failed three times. The punishment for this was Israel's sovereignty was removed from her, and she was put under the oppression of foreign countries for a specified number of years. In Luke 13:8, the vinedresser (the angel of the Lord—see chapter two) said they should leave the tree alone, and he would take care of it and do what it takes so the tree would bear fruit. In other words, Israel would be given a fourth opportunity to bear spiritual fruit. In Matthew 24:32 and verses 33–34, Jesus is using symbolic language to say that Israel will be reestablished as a sovereign nation, and at the same time he is also answering the disciple's question they asked earlier at the beginning of Matthew chapter twenty four.

The Disciples Question

The disciples asked Jesus in verse three, "What is the sign of your coming, and of the end of the age?" (Matthew 24:3c). The likely thought behind this question in verse three is, *when will Jesus, the man who performs miracles, deliver the people of Israel from Roman oppression?* They asked him this question (with this underlying thought) because this is all they had on their minds. The disciple's knowledge of future events was limited at this time. They also had the understanding that their Messiah king would deliver Israel from her enemies (see Psalms 44:7; 136:24). The disciples did not know at this point that Jesus was going to leave them. They could not foresee Jesus being crucified or even being raised from the dead then ascending back into heaven. But little did the disciples know their question was divinely inspired.

In their question is an actual prophetic query, which is, *What signs will there be on the Earth of Jesus's second coming and the end of the church age?* These are two distinct questions, and Jesus prophetically gives the answer to both in Matthew chapter twenty-four. In this chapter, along with the parallel passages in Mark and Luke, Jesus prophecies the time of his coming back to the earth to fulfill Daniel's prophecy, which is written in Daniel 9:24 and reads:

> Seventy weeks are decreed on your people and on your holy city, to finish disobedience, and to make an end of sins, and to make reconciliation for iniquity, and to bring in everlasting righteousness, and to seal up vision and prophecy, and to anoint the most holy.
>
> Daniel 9:24

This seventy-week period culminates with the second coming of the Messiah (Christ), who is the Most Holy. Some translations have interpreted Daniel 9:24 to refer to the most holy place, which is the holy of holies. But when Christ comes back to bring everlasting righteousness to Israel, Israel does not anoint the holy of holies but the one who reconciles them to their God. He is the Most Holy, who is their Messiah, the Anointed One.

Jesus also reveals in Matthew chapter twenty-four a clear indication of the end of the church age, which is the *catching away* of the bride of Christ.

KNOWLEDGE BEGETS MORE KNOWLEDGE

Jesus uses the analogy of the fig tree blossoming to reveal the time of his second coming. With the knowledge of the time of the second coming comes also the knowledge of the season of the catching away of the church. The second coming is when Jesus redeems Israel, and she will be finished with her disobedience never again be unfaithful to the LORD her God. She will never be referred to as the "fig tree" again in the negative sense because of being unfaithful for breaking the covenant of God. There is no mistaking what Christ is teaching in Matthew 24:27, 30–31. Jesus makes it clear that he is revealing the time of his second coming.

The LORD Jesus Christ is revealing to those who have ears to hear in Matthew 24:27–34 that his second coming will be witnessed by the *same generation* who sees Israel reestablished as a sovereign nation. Jesus says this also: "Most assuredly I tell you, this generation will not pass away, until all these things are accomplished" (Matthew 24:34). As the people in Jesus's day knew that when a literal fig tree blossoms that summer is near, likewise the people who witness the rebirth of Israel will know that the second coming of Christ is near. In fact, this latter group will know that his coming is right at the door (see Matthew 24:33). We also know this same generation that witnesses Israel's reestablishment and the second coming is the same generation that will also witness the catching away of the body of Christ.

ALL THE TREES

When we look in Luke chapter twenty-one, we see Luke writes this phrase: "See the fig tree and all the trees" (Luke 21:29). Luke not only writes that Jesus said in his parable to "see the fig tree," which refers to Israel, but to see "all the trees," which symbolically represents all the nations. In chapter two I discussed the parable of the man who planted a fig tree in his vineyard. I said that the term *tree* is also symbolically used in Scripture to represent the nations. Again, if you need to refresh your memory, you can check the example we looked at in Ezekiel 31:3–18.

The phrase "all the trees" in Luke's gospel symbolically represents the nations that relate to Israel prior to the second coming. They would be Russia, Iran, Syria, Lebanon, and most of the surrounding Arab nations. You can see these nations in Psalms chapter eighty-three and Ezekiel chapters thirty-eight and thirty-nine by their names at the time of these Old Testament prophecies. According to the prophetic word in Psalms chapter eighty-three and Ezekiel chapter thirty-eight and thirty-nine, these nations will come against Israel in an unsuccessful attempt to destroy her once Israel has been reestablished as a sovereign nation.

I do not know why Matthew and Mark do not include this news about these other nations, because this extra bit of information helps to reinforce the accuracy of Jesus's prophesies about his coming again. We know that all three writers were inspired to write what they wrote, but this also shows us how the Spirit of God works alongside the personality of each man. What I mean is that Luke included all the trees along with the fig tree because Jesus must have said it. The Holy Spirit would not inspire Luke to write something Jesus did not say. As far as I know, this phrase was not added in later on as manuscripts of the Gospel of Luke were being copied. The most likely scenario is that Dr. Luke, being a more educated man, would have paid closer attention to the little details like this. Luke might have studied the Hebrew prophets' writings of this future battle of the nations against Israel. So when Luke was researching his gospel and heard this news about "all the trees," he was inspired by the Spirit to add it, where the other two writers may not have been moved to do likewise.

OTHER SIGNS

We see also in Matthew chapter twenty-four that Jesus gives an extensive list of other events that will take place in this same generation. For example, many will claim they are the Messiah, there will be wars and rumors of wars, nations and kingdoms will rise up against each other, and there will be famines, plagues, and earthquakes in various places. Israel will be hated by all the nations, and Christians will be hated too, because they belong to Jesus Christ. Sin will be an exalted form of living, which will cause the hearts of people to think only of themselves. A man of political power will arise as the false Messiah, deceiving the people of Israel, and he will defile the temple as Daniel transcribed. The false prophet will show great signs and wonders, deceiving many, even Israel.

All these things and more will be witnessed by the generation who sees the second coming, with Israel's reestablishment as a sovereign nation being the primary event. It can be said that Israel's rebirth is the light that turns green that allows all these things to streak forward so the words of Jesus can come to fulfillment. Jesus pinpoints his coming with this statement from Matthew:

Even so you also, when you see all these things, know that it is near, even at the doors. Most assuredly I tell you, this generation will not pass away, until all these things are accomplished.

Matthew 24:33–34

WHAT IS A GENERATION?

Usually, when I talk to Christians about the day and the hour of the catching away, or the second coming, some seem to always ask how long a generation is. But Jesus was not attaching a specific number of years when he used the word *generation*. He was referring to the group of people living in the same time period of Israel's restoration. Pay particular attention to the language Jesus uses in these verses, especially with the phrase: "When you see all these things" (Matthew 24:33a). The word *see* in this phrase means more than to just see with the eyes. His primary purpose in using this phrase was not to refer to optical vision. But the primary intention of this phrase is to perceive with the mind or to understand the events taking place, in particular as the events surround the reestablishment of the Israeli Nation. So Jesus is quite literally saying, albeit in symbolic language, the people who saw and understood the events unfolding, in particular Israel being born in a day in May 1948 are the same people who will be alive to witness the second coming. Of course, it is understandable that many of these same people will pass on physically before this *day* takes place. But according to the Word of the LORD, there will be some who will still be alive to witness both events.

WHO KNEW ABOUT IT?

The news about the Jews forming their own nation in the land of Israel was international news in May 1948, so these questions come to my mind: Can a newborn baby understand what happened this day in May 1948? Can a five-year-old or a ten-year-old comprehend what was going on? Were their minds developed enough to be able to comprehend that their people were forming their own nation for the first time since they were exiled by the Babylonians?

Okay, let us say a ten-year-old was able to comprehend what was happening—that their nation was being reborn in a day. We take these same ten-year-olds, and if they live according to the average human life expectancy, which is seventy-nine to eighty years, then a portion of these same ten-year-olds who witnessed Israel's rebirth will still be alive to witness the second coming of Jesus Christ. I also need to add, that the *catching away* of those faithful to the LORD Jesus Christ precedes the second coming of Israel's Messiah by *at least seven biblical years* according to Daniel 9:24–27 and 2 Thessalonians 2:1–3, 5–7 (I explain later on). So I concede that the *day and the hour are sooner then we think!*

Daniel's Vision

The nation of Israel is a key player concerning the second coming of Christ. In fact, it is Israel that Jesus will come and rescue from the false messiah, who is doing all he can to destroy her. After Jesus Christ rescues Israel, he will in turn destroy the false messiah, as we read in 2 Thessalonians: "Whom the LORD will kill with the breath of his mouth, and bring to nothing by the brightness of his coming" (2 Thessalonians 2:8b). Jesus will then make an end to Israel's sins, and she will anoint Jesus as her Messiah and king. If you have not been paying attention to the nation of Israel in the world news you should be, because with each event surrounding her comes very important knowledge that all who love her should know. Christians need to pray for Israel with consistency, because they belong to God first, and we Gentiles were grafted into God's family second. They may not be acting like the righteousness of God at this present time, but they will be made righteous—when they are finished with disobedience—at the second coming. Let us take a look at the prophetic Word pertaining to Israel; beginning with Daniel's vision of the seventy weeks that are decreed for her.

The Vision

> Seventy weeks are decreed on your people and on your holy
> city, to finish disobedience, and to make an end of sins, and
> to make reconciliation for iniquity, and to bring in everlast-
> ing righteousness, and to seal up vision and prophecy, and to
> anoint the most holy. Know therefore and discern that from
> the going forth of the mitzvah [commandment] to restore
> and to build Yerushalayim [Jerusalem] to the Messiah the
> prince, shall be seven weeks, and sixty-two weeks: it shall
> be built again, with street and moat, even in troubled times.
> After the sixty-two weeks the Anointed One shall be cut
> off, and shall have nothing: and the people of the prince
> who shall come shall destroy the city and the sanctuary;
> and the end of it shall be with a flood, and even to the end
> shall be war; desolations are determined. He shall make a
> firm covenant with many for one week: and in the midst
> of the week he shall cause the sacrifice and the offering to
> cease; and on the wing of abominations [shall come] one
> who makes desolate; and even to the full end, and that
> determined, shall [wrath] be poured out on the desolate.
>
> Daniel 9:24–27

In Daniel 9:20–21, we read that while Daniel is in prayer,
the angel Gabriel comes to him and gives him this message from
God in the form of a vision. It is the Word of God to Daniel
of the precise time of Christ's first coming to present himself
as king, and a second and final time to present himself as king
again.

The time of this visitation is around the year 539 BC, and
Israel has been in exile to Babylon for approximately sixty-seven
to sixty-eight biblical years. Daniel has learned through read-

ing the writings of the Prophet Jeremiah that Israel's captivity would be seventy biblical years. Jeremiah prophecies, "This whole land shall be desolation, and astonishment; and these nations shall serve the king of Bavel [Babylon] seventy years" (Jeremiah 25:11). Daniel would have also read what the prophet wrote in chapter twenty-nine: "For thus says the LORD, 'After seventy years are accomplished for Bavel [Babylon], I will visit you, and perform my good word toward you, in causing you to return to this place'" (Jeremiah 29:10).

THE EXILE

The Babylonian Empire exiled the first deportees of the remnant of Judah, who escaped the sword in 605 BC under the leadership of Nebuchadnezzar (see 2 Chronicles 36:5–8; Daniel 1:1–2). While Israel was held in captivity to the Babylonians, the Mede-Persian Empire overtook Babylon in 539 BC. About one year after this, Cyrus, the king of Persia, makes a proclamation because the LORD had stirred up his spirit that the Jews were allowed to leave Babylon freely to go build the house of the LORD, which is in Jerusalem (see 2 Chronicles 36:22–23; Ezra 1:1–5). The LORD began to move the hearts of the chief fathers of the tribes of Judah and Benjamin, along with the priests and Levites and some others, to go back to Jerusalem to rebuild the temple. By the time the last portion of this group of returnees left Babylon to rebuild the temple it was April, 536 BC.

So the Jews spent an approximate number of seventy biblical years as captives in a land that was not their own. There were less then 50,000 Jews who left Babylon at this time, while millions of Jews remained in the Persian Empire, in which they conveniently blended in with the Persian culture. The reason why the years 605 BC to 536 BC only add up to sixty-nine years and not seventy years is because Israel was exiled seventy biblical years, which are lunar years, and we are using dates from the solar calendar. Any time the Bible speaks about a number of years, it always refers to lunar years, which are a 360-day period and not a solar year, which we in our contemporary world are accustomed to. The difference between seventy lunar years verses seventy solar years is approximately 367 days, which gives the lunar calendar a full-year increase over the solar calendar. So when Jeremiah said that Israel would be exiled in Babylon for seventy years, he meant seventy lunar years, which total sixty-nine solar years.

- 360 days in a lunar year
- 365.24219 days in a solar year

GABRIEL'S PROPHECY

Gabriel initially came by the command of God to give Daniel wisdom and understanding concerning the future of the nation of Israel. This wisdom and understanding was not limited to Daniel alone, for his writings were to be passed down to the succeeding generations, which they were. The spiritual leaders of Israel, when Jesus was fulfilling his earthly ministry, had access to Gabriel's prophecy through Daniel's writings. When Jesus came to Israel the first time, riding on the back of a donkey, that generation should have known through the prophets, especially Daniel 9:24–26, that he was their Messiah King. But because of jealousy and competition, it caused them to be blind, as it says in Matthew chapter thirteen:

> In them the prophecy of Yesha`yahu [Isaiah] is fulfilled, which says, 'By hearing you will hear, And will in no way

understand; Seeing you will see, And will in no way perceive: / For this people's heart has grown callous, Their ears are dull of hearing, They have closed their eyes; Or else perhaps they might perceive with their eyes, Hear with their ears, Understand with their heart, And should turn again; And I would heal them.'

Matthew 13:14–15

We in this generation have the same writings of the prophets, and in particular, this same prophecy given to Daniel just as Israel's spiritual leaders had in their generation, but there is no pressure on us to recognize Jesus as the Messiah like they had. We do not have the same pressure they had, because we have the letters of the new covenant to help us believe. Even one who is a Jew growing up in the Jewish faith in this age of the church can read the New Testament and the blindness will be lifted from their eyes, unlike the stubborn leaders of Israel in that day. If you are not sure that Jesus is LORD, and likewise are not sure he was raised from the dead, then I encourage you to read the New Testament. Gabriel told Daniel to understand the vision that was given to him, and likewise God will help you to understand the New Testament.

Gabriel says there are seventy weeks decreed on the people of Israel and Jerusalem. It says this in Daniel chapter nine:

Seventy weeks are decreed on your people and on your holy city, to finish disobedience, and to make an end of sins, and to make reconciliation for iniquity, and to bring in everlasting righteousness, and to seal up vision and prophecy, and to anoint the most holy.

Daniel 9:24

The seventy weeks are prophetic language referring to seventy multiply seven biblical years, which total 490 biblical years. To understand this prophecy, along with any biblical prophecy, it is important to think in lunar years and then convert the time into solar years. Some interpreters, especially in the past, have not thought in lunar years when trying to interpret biblical prophecy (they just thought in solar years), and as a consequence, they have found themselves all confused because dates don't line up for them. I thank the LORD, though, as the day and the hour of the catching away of the bride of Christ approaches even closer, that the Spirit of God is helping us to interpret prophesies with even more accuracy.

This prophetic word to Daniel says that after the seventy weeks (490 biblical years) have been complete, Israel will be finished with her stubborn rebellion against God, and they will anoint their Messiah in the holy city of Jerusalem. We Christians know this event more commonly as the second coming of the LORD, Jesus Christ, when Jesus returns to the earth and establishes his millennium kingdom, with the holy city of Jerusalem being the capital city of his kingdom. No wonder there is so much conflict right now over this holy city, because Jerusalem is the most important city on this planet. This period will begin a new era in Israel's existence. When, for the first time, Israel will live in everlasting righteousness under the authority of her long-awaited king, as Israel will finally be reconciled to her God. God loves this nation so much, even though Israel has tested his love for her for at least 3,500 years, and as a result, she has suffered so much because of her disobedience.

ARTAXERXES' DECREE

As we continue with this prophecy, Gabriel says to Daniel:

> Know therefore and discern, that from the going forth
> of the mitzvah [commandment] to restore and to build
> Yerushalayim [Jerusalem] to the Messiah the prince, shall
> be seven weeks, and sixty-two weeks: it shall be built again,
> with street and moat, even in troubled times.
>
> Daniel 9:25

Gabriel gives Daniel this word with precise accuracy. Daniel
is actually receiving from Gabriel the exact time of Israel's first
visitation of her Messiah King in this verse. From the "going
forth of the mitzvah [commandment]" (Daniel 9:25a) refers to
the granting of Nehemiah's request, issued by King Artaxerxes,
to rebuild Jerusalem and its walls (see Nehemiah 2:1–9). King
Artaxerxes reigned as king in Persia from approximately 465 to
424 BC. The prophet Nehemiah says this was in the Jewish month
of Nisan, which is the first month of the Jewish New Year, in the
twentieth year of King Artaxerxes reign. The Jewish Talmud,
though, is a little more detailed and says this day occurred on the
first day of Nisan, while Bible theologian Sir Robert Anderson
(1841–1918), confirms this date also in chapter ten of his book
entitled *The Coming Prince*. Sir Robert Anderson also calculates
the first day of Nisan as March 14, 445 BC on the Julian calendar,
in his same book and chapter.[2]

TIME CALCULATED

As said, the Jewish month of Nisan is the first month of the Jewish
calendar, and it falls during our March or April period, according to the positioning of the moon. This commandment, which

was issued by the king of Persia to restore and build Jerusalem (see Daniel 9:25), is the starting point of the seventy weeks (490 biblical years) decreed on Israel and the Holy City of Jerusalem (see Daniel 9:24). Some modern Bible scholars have calculated dates within a year or two of Sir Robert Anderson's calculation (March 14, 445 BC), but you will see with the formula used to calculate the days between when the decree was given to rebuild Jerusalem to when Christ was rejected, March 14, 445 BC, is the more plausible date. I am not using Sir Robert Anderson's calculations because I did my own. I do not even know if his and my calculations are the same because I never even looked at his. When I did my arithmetic for the following calculations, I kept my attention off of Sir Roberts's work so as not to be influenced by his calculations. I wanted to make sure, for myself, that my calculations fit the March fourteenth date like his. I used the same starting base, March 14, 445 BC, as he did, because of his research findings from the Royal Observatory in Greenwich, London, England (*The Coming Prince*).[3] If Sir Robert, who was not only a great Bible theologian but also the assistant commissioner of the crime unit at Scotland Yard, came up with this date for the first day of Nisan using his police skills, then *who* should argue with him? This date of March 14, 445 BC, is ninety-one solar years after King Cyrus of Persia ordered the temple to be rebuilt and allowed the Jews to go back to Jerusalem to begin their work on the second temple in 536 BC (see 2 Chronicles 36:22–23; Ezra 1:1–5). The completion of the second temple was completed between 516 and 515 BC.

Daniel 9:25 also says that from the time the commandment is given to restore and to rebuild Jerusalem, there will be "seven weeks" plus "sixty-two weeks" until the Messiah comes. Gabriel was still using prophetic language as he was conversing with

Daniel, and his prophetic word interprets the "seven and sixty-two weeks" like this: Seven multiply seven biblical years, plus sixty-two multiply seven biblical years, which figure to forty-nine and 434 biblical years. When we total the two numbers, we get a grand total of 483 biblical years until Jesus presents himself to Israel as their Messiah King.

- 7 multiply 7 = 49 biblical years

- 62 multiply 7 = 434 biblical years

- 49 + 434 = 483 biblical years

When we break the 483 biblical years down into days, we get a total of 173,880 days from the time the commandment was given to restore Jerusalem until the Messiah presents himself to the people of Israel.

- 483 multiply 360 = 173,880 days

In this same verse, it says Jerusalem "will be built again, with street and moat," which means the city will be allowed to function as a normal city, with a public works department. It goes on to say that Jerusalem will be built "even in troubled times," which suggests there will be stiff opposition to the restoration and building of the city. If you read Nehemiah 4:6, you will see that Sanballat the Horonite, Tobiah the Ammonite, and others gave the Jews a lot of trouble as they began to repair the walls; but God was with Israel, and the work was completed.

The Christ is Cut Off

In Daniel 9:26, Gabriel breaks down this prophecy to Daniel, saying that after the sixty-two weeks, the Christ "will be cut off, and shall have nothing." This is what we read in verse twenty-six:

> After the sixty-two weeks, the Anointed One shall be cut off, and shall have nothing: and the people of the prince who shall come shall destroy the city and the sanctuary; and the end of it shall be with a flood, and even to the end shall be war; desolations are determined.
>
> Daniel 9:26

The phrase "have nothing" means that Jesus will not be crowned the king of Israel at this point. We do know that Jesus Christ will be crowned King at the end of Israel's seventy-week period, when Israel will anoint the Most Holy One as their Messiah King. "After the sixty-two week period" refers to the full 483 biblical years being completed.

Why did Gabriel break up the sixty-nine week period into seven weeks and sixty-two weeks to begin with? God would not instruct Gabriel to give Daniel this prophetic word in such a complicated fashion without a reason. Our LORD does not use his words to form sentences frivolously, or he would not say that everyone will give an account for every idle word we speak. I believe the reason why this prophecy was given this way is because much happened in Israel during the first seven-week period, which is the first forty-nine biblical years of this prophecy.

First, the walls of the city were completed a little over a year and a half after the decree was given on March 14, 445 BC, to restore and to rebuild Jerusalem. According to Nehemiah 6:15, it took Nehemiah and the men of Israel fifty-two days to complete the building of the walls in spite of the opposition. But it took approximately between the years 397 and 396 BC for the men of Israel to complete the rebuild of Jerusalem. This is forty-nine biblical years after the commandment was given to rebuild

Jerusalem. It is also believed that around this time period, the silent years began, in which there were no prophets giving words to Israel from God.

- 49 biblical years = 17,640 days
- March 14, 445 BC plus 49 biblical years = approximately June 30, 397 BC

The prophetic word continues with the prediction that "the Anointed One, shall be cut off" (Daniel 9:26a), which refers to Jesus Christ being rejected by Israel as their Messiah King. The LORD, Jesus Christ, came and presented himself as their Messiah King on *Palm Sunday,* and the *religious and political* leaders of the Jewish nation rejected him.

When we look at the narrative of Palm Sunday in Luke 19:29–44, we see the LORD Jesus riding into Jerusalem on the back of a donkey colt. The disciples of Jesus, plus many others whom he had taught, were throwing their cloaks down on the ground for Jesus to ride over, shouting praises to God for the works that Jesus had done. Luke chapter nineteen reports the disciples of Jesus were saying, "Blessed is the King who comes in the name of the LORD! Shalom [peace] in heaven, and glory in the highest!" (Luke 19:38). But Israel's religious leaders demanded Jesus reprimand his shouting disciples, which is clear indication of their *unbelief and rejection* of Christ's authority. When Jesus drew near to the city of Jerusalem, he wept over it because the people of Israel "didn't know the time of their visitation" (Luke 19:44b). Just as Gabriel had told Daniel "the Anointed One shall be cut off, and shall have nothing" (Daniel 9:26a), Israel, through her religious leaders, cut the Most Holy off from becoming their Messiah King on the day of the visitation.

THE VISITATION

The date of this visitation is April 06, AD 32. This day is the beginning of the same week when Christ was hung on the tree and crucified. There are many conflicting dates concerning the day, but the most credible ones are within a year of AD 32. Even if some have calculated dates within two or, at the most, three years from AD 32, I personally would not argue with them over that. But I will make an argument for the dates that the Gospel of Luke records, because Luke gives us evidence of the *exact year* Jesus began his ministry, which was the *same year* John the Baptist began his. Then from this we can pretty well determine the year of Christ's visitation.

Luke says in chapter 3:1–3, that the Word of God came to John the Baptist, and he began his preaching ministry, which was in the fifteenth year of Tiberius Caesar. Luke chapter three verses twenty-one through twenty-three implies that in this same year, Jesus began his ministry once he was baptized by John. It says Jesus was about the age of thirty, which means he was at least thirty years of age and no younger, because Jews were not allowed to be rabbis until they reached the age of thirty in Jesus's day. Tiberius Caesar was not officially coronated as sole emperor of Rome until his predecessor, Julius Caesar Augustus, passed away in August, AD 14. Prior to this date of August, AD 14, Tiberius was co-emperor with Julius Caesar Augustus from AD 11 until mid September, AD 13, when Tiberius assumed full power because Julius Caesar was too ill to co-reign. As said, Tiberius did not assume position as sole Emperor, in which he held the title of Augustus until the Roman senate approved him in mid August, AD 14, after Emperor Julius Caesar Augustus died.

Augustus was the title given to each Roman emperor after Julius Caesar Augustus to give *recognition* that all the powers of Julius Caesar were passed on to his successors. The title "Augustus" was given to each Roman emperor at his coronation, in which this title has the meaning of majesty. When Luke says that Jesus and John did not begin their ministries until the fifteenth year of Tiberius Caesar, we would assume that Luke was using as a starting point for this said year, the year Tiberius assumed *full control* of Rome, which was mid September of AD 13, even though Tiberius was not designated Augustus until August, AD 14. In the year AD 13, when Tiberius assumed full control of Rome, he was appointed with the title of Caesar, which is a title inherited from Julius Caesar (as is the title of Augustus). But again, the title of Augustus is not given until the Caesar is coronated. In AD 13, Tiberius would have only had the title of Caesar and not Caesar Augustus, which came a year later, in AD 14. Thus, this is likely why Luke used the title Tiberius Caesar only—instead of Tiberius Caesar Augustus—when he recorded chapter three of his gospel. So it is only logical that Luke would begin counting the fifteen years of Tiberius Caesars reign from the year AD 13, when he assumed the power and title of Caesar.

When we do the math, using as a starting point of mid September AD 13, and add the fifteen-biblical-year period as Luke reports in chapter 3:1–3, we arrive at an approximate date of any time after June 28, AD 28, in which the ministry of John and Jesus began. The reason for this calculation is that Luke is not specific to the month and day in Tiberius's fifteenth year. Taking the approximate day of September 15, AD 13, when Tiberius assumed full control of Rome, and adding a minimum of fifteen biblical years, which total 5,400 days, we arrive at date of June 28, AD 28. Since Luke says it was in the fifteenth year of

Tiberius's reign, then any time after this date in June is when the ministries of John the Baptist and Jesus the Christ began.

- September 15, AD 13, plus 5,400 days (15 biblical years) = June 28, AD 28

CALCULATIONS: TO THE TIME OF THE CUT OFF

Again, as the prophecy says in Daniel, from the going forth of the commandment to restore and build Jerusalem, to when the Messiah comes and is rejected, will be seven weeks plus sixty-two weeks, which total 483 biblical years. As we discussed this date, the commandment went forth March 14, 445 BC, and the date the Messiah was cut off was April 6, AD 32. Between these two dates there are a total of 173,880 days, which when divided by 360 days, gives us a total of 483 lunar years. This is the exact number of years the Book of Daniel says there will be from the going forth of the commandment to the cutting off of the Anointed One.

To help you confirm the number of days between March 14, 445 BC, and April 6, AD 32, we must convert the time into solar years. The solar years between March 14, 445 BC, and March 14, AD 32, are 476 solar years.

- 445 + 32=477 solar years

We then have to minus one year from this figure of 477 solar years, because there is only one year between one BC and AD 1, because there is no such year as Zero BC or AD Zero. If there were such a year as Zero BC or AD Zero, then there would be two years between 1 BC and AD 1 (but there is neither year). So now the figure is 476 solar years between March 14, 445 BC, and March 14, AD 32.

- 477–1 = 476 solar years

Now we multiply 476 solar years by the number of days in a solar year, which is 365.24219, and we get a total of 173,855.28244 solar days.

- 476 multiply 365.24219 = 173,855.28244 solar days

Then we take the number of solar days (173,855.28244) and minus the number of days we derived from 483 lunar years, which was 173,880 lunar days, and we get a difference of 24.71756 days. This figure comes to twenty-four days and approximately fifteen hours.

- 173,855.28244 solar days - 173,880 lunar days = 24.71756 days
- 24 days + approximately 15 hours

Then we add the days between March 14, AD 32, to April 6, AD 32, and we get a sum total of twenty-four days, including April 6.

Now we add the 173,855.28244 solar days, plus the twenty-four days from March 14 to April 6, and we get 173,879.28244 days.

- 173,855.28244 solar days + 24 days = 173,879.28244 days

When we subtract the 173,879.28244 days from the 173,880 days, we get a difference of just a little more than thirteen hours.

- 173,879.28244 days - 173,880 days = 13 hours.

Now I can be off by a few hours, but when we are talking 173,880 *days*, a few hours is insignificant.

I know this sounds a little complicated (it was for me doing the math), but in the end we have the seven weeks plus the sixty-two weeks, which are 483 biblical years, which total 173,880 days between the times the commandment was issued and the cutting-off of the Messiah, as the book of Daniel prophesied so accurately in chapter nine verses twenty five and twenty six.

THE EVIL PRINCE

I think it is also important to explain what Gabriel meant when he said to Daniel that, "The people of the prince who shall come shall destroy the city and the sanctuary" (Daniel 9:26). The "prince who shall come" refers to the *Antichrist,* and the "people of the prince" refers to his descendants, meaning the Romans. These people today are the European Union, which is the revived Roman Empire. The Antichrist will be the man who, very soon, will be the dictatorial leader of the European Union and its allies. His descendants back in AD 70, when they were known as the Roman Empire, destroyed the city of Jerusalem and the second temple, in which *millions* of people perished. This horrific event was predicted in the prophecy of Gabriel to Daniel (see Daniel 9:26), and Jesus also mentions it in Matthew chapter twenty-four: "But he answered them, 'Don't you see all of these things? Most assuredly I tell you, there will not be left here one stone on another that will not be thrown down'" (Matthew 24:2). This is about thirty-eight years after Israel's religious and political leaders rejected Jesus, their Messiah King. I suggest if you have not read the text, *Josephus the Essential Works,* by Dr. Paul L. Maier, that you do so. He is a brilliant teacher of ancient Jewish and Middle Eastern history, whom I have loved to listen to when he has been on *100 Huntley Street* (a popular Christian television program in Canada). In the textual work of Dr. Maier, he translates and edits Josephus's writings of this terrible time in Jewish history.

This leader of the European Union, whom I mentioned, will make a covenant with the people of Israel for one week, which refers to a period of seven biblical years, which is a total period of 2,520 days. We read this in Daniel also:

> He shall make a firm covenant with many for one week: and in the midst of the week he shall cause the sacrifice and the offering to cease; and on the wing of abominations [shall come] one who makes desolate; and even to the full end, and that determined, shall [wrath] be poured out on the desolate.
>
> Daniel 9:27

This one-week period is the final week of the seventy-week period prophesied in Daniel 9:24. The main point of this covenant is that the European Union and their illustrious leader will guarantee Israel and its people protection from those nations who desire to destroy her. This covenant will cause Israel to be deceived into believing this powerful man is their long-awaited Messiah. Israel is most likely near exhaustion because of all she has endured during this generation, especially in these latter years leading up to this agreement with the man of sin. Ever since Israel was reestablished in 1948, she has not had any rest. Nations and people groups that surround Israel from her reestablishment until now have given her nothing but trouble. If you listen to sincere Jews today, you will hear that they are longing for their Messiah King to come, as they should be. Israel is tired and are looking to anyone who will bring them peace.

But the nation of Israel receives the wrong messiah at the beginning of the seventieth week. Israel rejected Jesus the first time in AD 32, which was good for us Gentiles, so we who once were far from God could be brought near to him through the blood of Israel's Messiah King, our LORD, Jesus Christ (see Romans 11:11–12). Because the seventieth week was interrupted by Israel's rejection of their true Messiah after the sixty-ninth week, there have been over 1978 solar years in between the sixty-ninth week and the seventieth week (at the time of the writing of this book; it is the year 2010, and on the Jewish calendar it is the year 5770). This figures to be approximately a little over 2,006 biblical years since Israel rejected Jesus as their Messiah.

The prophetic word in the book of Daniel is precise in its prediction of Israel's first sixty-nine weeks, with Jesus coming to Israel and being cut off. It will be just as precise with its prediction of all the events of Israel's seventieth week, with the false messiah coming and making a covenant with Israel. This seventieth-week period is about to begin, because this is the generation that will experience Israel's seventieth week, as we discussed in chapter four.

Israel Reestablished

As we discussed in chapter four (*The Fig Tree Teaches a Parable*), the generation of people who were living at the time Israel was reestablished as a sovereign nation in 1948 and able to comprehend this event at least at some level will *be alive to witness* the Christ at his second coming. This will be at the end of Israel's seventieth-week period, prophesied in Daniel chapter nine:

> Seventy weeks are decreed on your people and on your holy city, to finish disobedience, and to make an end of sins, and to make reconciliation for iniquity, and to bring in everlasting righteousness, and to seal up vision and prophecy, and to anoint the most holy.
>
> Daniel 9:24

These people, along with the hundreds of millions who were born after 1948 and survive the seventieth week period of Israel, will not only witness the LORD, Jesus Christ, coming out of the heavens on a white horse, but they will witness at least seven biblical years previously, the *catching away* of the body of Christ from this earthly realm. Now I must say that each and every individual who witnessed the rebirth of the nation of Israel, whether Jew or Gentile, have every opportunity to put their faith in Jesus Christ as their LORD now, before the seventieth-week period begins. If they do put their faith in Jesus and not break his new covenant but continue to be faithful to him until the end, they will surely be among those who are caught up from this earthly realm to meet Jesus in the air. Anyone can do this by receiving this message written in 1 Corinthians: "That Messiah [Christ] died for our sins according to the Scriptures, that he was buried, that he was raised on the third day according to the Scriptures" (1 Corinthians 15:3b-4). This is putting faith in the person of Jesus Christ, the LORD, and what he has done for you. God the Father's plan for man to be redeemed is written in Romans chapter ten:

> If you will confess with your mouth the LORD Yeshua [Jesus], and believe in your heart that God raised him from the dead, you will be saved. For with the heart, one believes unto righteousness; and with the mouth confession is made unto salvation.
>
> Romans 10:9–10

The Apostle Paul said to receive the message I quoted above in 1 Corinthians and you will be saved, "if you hold firmly the word" (1 Corinthians 15:1–2). So *receive it* and *never let go of it* through turning again to a heart of unbelief.

I AM CONVINCED

You may have a different opinion on end-time theology, which is fine. This book is not written to discuss the many different theologies pertaining to the catching away or the second coming. I am *personally convinced* the Scriptures teach that the body of Christ will be *caught up* and taken out of this earthly realm, prior to the tribulation period, which is actually the seventieth week of Israel. I see the catching away of the body of Christ and the events that unfold after this event being pictured in the person of John the Apostle in the vision he saw beginning in Revelation chapter four. I see also in 1 Thessalonians 4:13–18 and 1 Corinthians 15:50–54 what the body of Christ will experience the moment the catching away is taking place, which *precedes* the seventieth week.

In the seventieth week, Revelation 11:12 says there will also be a catching away from the earth of the two Jewish witnesses. In Revelation 14:1–5, we see what looks like another catching away of the 144,000 who were sealed of all the tribes of the children of Israel (see Revelation 7:1–8). In the Old Testament, there are descriptions of certain people being *caught up* from the earth, namely both Elijah, the prophet, and Enoch, the man who had been well pleasing to God. This same Enoch, before he was *caught away,* had visions from God in which he saw the second coming of Christ, so he prophesied this statement, which was written in the letter of Jude: "See, the LORD is coming with thousands upon thousands of his holy ones" (Jude 1:14). The LORD Jesus was even caught up from the earth to heaven in Acts chapter one. So, there have been already and will be many more people who will experience a catching away from the earth's physical realm and a supernatural transport to heaven by the power of God.

In this chapter entitled *Israel Reestablished* I will present some interesting facts and figures that pertain to the reestablishment of the nation of Israel. From these facts and figures we can establish the approximate time of the second coming along with the season of the catching away of the body of Christ.

Always Be Led by the Holy Spirit!

Before we go any further, I need to remind you of something very important. What is so important is that you are seeking the Lord concerning this material you are reading in *The Day and the Hour*. Is what you are reading witnessing with your spirit by the spirit of Christ? If it is, then I encourage you to continue with your reading. Always seek the Lord whenever reading literary material purporting to be from the Bible. Does the literature line up with the Word of God? Sometimes we have to do a *little digging* into the Word of God yourself instead of just trusting the person who says it is from God. I ask everyone to sincerely read the scriptures I am presenting to *personally back up* what I am writing, especially as we get further along, because many things you will be reading will challenge your thoughts and ideas. Do you go through this process of testing the spirits when you hear your pastor or Bible teacher? You know we are commanded to do this according to what John wrote in his first letter, which says, "Beloved, don't believe every spirit, but test the spirits, whether they are of God, because many false prophets have gone out into the world" (1 John 4:1). This also applies to the material one is teaching, as well as the spirit behind the teaching. Remember, the Holy Spirit is here to "Guide you into all truth" (John 16:13).

What was the Hold-up?

Have you ever wondered why it took so long for Israel to be reestablished as a sovereign nation? Did God forget about Israel and then all of a sudden in the twentieth century decide to bring her back to the land that he gave her? There is a very good reason why Israel was not reestablished until the year 1948. It had to do with a time of punishment imposed on Israel by her God for her *continual* disobedience. It was Israel's disobedience to the word of the LORD that brought this punishment on them. I personally had never heard of any length of punishment before until I read the book entitled, *Armageddon, Appointment with Destiny,* by Dr. Grant Jeffrey.[4] The information that Dr. Jeffery writes in his book interested me greatly, so I looked into the Scriptures and did some research on my own to see if his research lined up with Scripture (which of course, I should). Although some of my findings may not be exactly like Dr. Jeffery's research, he is the one to receive the credit for what everyone reads about the revelation of the length of Israel's punishment in chapter six. As far as I know, God opened up Dr. Jeffery's spiritual eyes and gave him understanding into this mystery before anyone else. It was from Dr. Jeffrey's work that God lead me into the mysteries of his Word concerning the length of Israel's punishment and revealed to me what I have written.

In chapter two (*The Fig Tree*), we discussed both the northern and southern kingdoms of Israel being taken into captivity by foreign nations. In 722 BC, the northern kingdom, also known as Samaria, was taken into captivity by King Shalmaneser of Assyria. Assyria, during this time, was known as the Neo-Assyrian Empire, which succeeded Old and Middle Assyria. The Neo-Assyrian Empire later became part of the Neo-Babylonian Empire, which began to exile the southern kingdom of Israel in 605 BC. In the late years of the southern kingdom's exile, both Assyria and Babylon became part of the Persian Empire. Today these geographical areas are known as Iraq and Iran.

Neo-Assyria besieged the northern kingdom of Israel for three years, until the year 722 BC when their king overtook Israel and exiled Samaria. The reason why the northern kingdom of Israel was exiled into this foreign land was because they were *consistently unfaithful* to the LORD their God. The writer of 2 Kings, who was likely the prophet Jeremiah, writes this:

> For [so] it was, that the children of Israel had sinned against the LORD their God, who had brought them out of the land of Egypt, from under the hand of Pharaoh king of Egypt, and had feared other gods, And walked in the statutes of the heathen, whom the LORD cast out from before the children of Israel, and of the kings of Israel which they had made.
>
> 2 Kings 17:7–8 (Webster's Bible)

As said, the southern kingdom of Israel, known as Judah, had its first group of deportees exiled by the Neo-Babylonian Empire under the leadership of King Nebuchadnezzar in 605 BC. In this year, Nebuchadnezzar began to deport the choice of Judah's stock to a land that was not their own, because just like her sister, Samaria, Judah was *unfaithful* to her God. It says also in 2 Kings: "Also Yehudah [Judah] didn't keep the mitzvot [commandment] of the LORD their God, but walked in the statutes of Yisra'el [Israel] which they made" (2 Kings 17:19). The LORD rejected both kingdoms (of Israel), casting them from his sight on two separate occasions, delivering both Samaria and Judah into the hands of foreign nations.

Since the year 605 BC, the reign of King David's descendants upon the throne of Israel came to an end until David's greatest descendant, our LORD Jesus Christ will once again sit on David's throne. This will begin to take place after Israel's seventieth-week period is finished. The nation of Israel as a whole, both the northern and southern kingdoms, ceased to be a self-governing body of people until Israel's reestablishment in the year 1948.

THE REASON FOR REJECTION

Israel was rejected by the LORD because of their *persistent unfaithfulness* to him and his commands as we read here: "The LORD rejected all the seed of Yisra'el [Israel], and afflicted them, and delivered them into the hand of spoilers, until he had cast them out of his sight" (2 Kings 17:20). The phrase "he had cast them out of his sight" (2 Kings 17:20c) is symbolic language for *they would be removed from the LORD's presence.* This meant that the nations to whom Israel would be subjected to from this point on could do whatever they wanted to do with them. If the nations Israel were subjected to choose to allow them to live in relative peace and freedom and allowed them to live within their own culture and to work and make their own living like the Babylonians and the Persians did, then that was fine. On the other hand, if the nations Israel were subjected to like the Romans, who were the "people of the prince who shall come" (Daniel 9:26b) chose to slaughter Israel, as history tells us, then this would be Israel's plight. There were millions of Jews brutally murdered by the Romans in AD 70 as Rome destroyed both Jerusalem and the second temple.

These examples were the result of the LORD casting Israel out of his sight. But before Israel was cast out of the LORD's sight, Israel received the LORD's protection from foreign nations. The responsibility for being cast out of the LORD's sight was on the part of Israel because of her unfaithfulness in spite of many warnings. Of course, the individual Israelite could call on the name of the LORD, and he would save them from harm. Case and point would be Shadrach, Meshach, and Abednego, who were delivered without harm when thrown into the burning fiery furnace, and likewise Daniel, who was also delivered without harm when cast into the den of hungry lions. When we read

Daniel chapters three and six we see that God delivered all four of these men because they remained faithful to the LORD. This does not mean that those who have been killed for the LORD's sake were not faithful to him. On the contrary, these people were given the highest honor in the kingdom of God, which is to die at the hands of evil men for the Word of the LORD.

As a nation, Israel would be cast from the LORD's sight until the LORD could deal with them for their persistent unfaithfulness. The LORD dealt with Israel for her sin by punishing her and taking away her independence and making her subject to foreign nations. Usually, as with any punishment, the judge hands down a specified amount of time when one is found guilty of an offense; this is part of any court ruling. In Israel's case, the LORD handed down a specific amount of time of punishment for her continued unfaithfulness. The government of the kingdom operates with laws, and within these laws there is punishment for unfaithfulness. If the kingdom of God does not hold fast to its laws within it, the kingdom itself will crumble because it is held together by God's Word. And God, by his Word, has set up laws within his kingdom to make it function. That is why Jesus had to take *our sins* upon his *own body*, because of one of the laws within the kingdom, which read: "According to the law, nearly everything is cleansed with blood, and apart from shedding of blood there is no remission" (Hebrews 9:22). In Israel's case, her punishment was brought on by disobedience, because punishment is not administered if the law is not broken. Again, Israel's punishment for unfaithfulness would be for a specified amount of time. It would be a specific number of years where Israel would be subject to other nations and Israel would have to do what these nations told her to do.

The Punishment

We see in the writings of the prophet Ezekiel the number of years handed down to Israel as punishment for her persistent unfaithfulness to the LORD. Ezekiel was exiled with a second group of Israelites to the nation of Babylon, about eight years after Daniel and his group was exiled. Ezekiel received many words from the LORD pertaining to Israel while he was there. If you have never studied (or haven't in a while) the writings of Ezekiel, I encourage you to do so. Ezekiel was a very intelligent Jewish man who seemed to know much about everything.

The LORD called Ezekiel to speak to the children of Israel, whether they listened to him or not, and he commanded Ezekiel not to be afraid of them or their words or even the looks they give him. The LORD had to make Ezekiel's forehead and face hard against the foreheads and faces of the Israelites, because the LORD knew Israel would not listen to the word of the LORD spoken through Ezekiel. This is precisely why the house of Israel was in exile, because they would not listen to the word of the LORD. We see in Ezekiel the length of punishment handed down to Israel by God through the prophet:

> You also, son of man, take a tile, and lay it before you, and portray on it a city, even Yerushalayim [Jerusalem]: and lay siege against it, and build forts against it, and cast up a mound against it; set camps also against it, and plant battering rams against it round about. Take for yourself an iron pan, and set it for a wall of iron between you and the city: and set your face toward it, and it shall be besieged, and you shall lay siege against it. This shall be a sign to the house of Yisra'el [Israel]. Moreover lie you on your left side, and lay the iniquity of the house of Yisra'el [Israel] on it; [according to] the number of the days that you shall lie on it, you shall

bear their iniquity. For I have appointed the years of their iniquity to be to you a number of days, even three hundred ninety days: so shall you bear the iniquity of the house of Yisra'el [Israel]. Again, when you have accomplished these, you shall lie on your right side, and shall bear the iniquity of the house of Yehudah [Judah]: forty days, each day for a year, have I appointed it to you.

Ezekiel 4:1–6

This passage tells us that God instructed Ezekiel to act out his prophetic word to Israel, as he does at other times in Ezekiel's calling. Israel's length of punishment is acted out by Ezekiel by him lying on both sides of his body, as per instruction of the LORD. First Ezekiel is to lie on his left side, to bear the iniquity of the house of Israel, which refers to the northern kingdom. He is to lie on his left side for 390 days while he bears Israel's iniquity, which God will appoint one year for each day. Then Ezekiel is to lie on his right side for forty days to bear the iniquity of the house of Judah, which refers to the southern kingdom. Here also, for each day Ezekiel bears Judah's iniquity, God will appoint each day as equaling one year.

In total, Ezekiel laid on both sides of his body for 430 days, bearing the iniquity of both kingdoms, which God appointed for each day a year. This prophetic word means Israel will be punished for her iniquities for a total of 430 years.

- 390 days lying on his left side: figures to 390 years (each day represents one year)
- 40 days lying on his right side: figures to 40 years (each day represents one year)
- 390 + 40 = 430 biblical years

The starting date for this punishment was 605 BC, when Judah was captured by King Nebuchadnezzar of the Neo-Babylonian Empire. King Nebuchadnezzar made Jehoiakim, the king of Judah, subservient to him and began to deport Israel into exile to Babylon on this date. This was the last of the great Israeli Empire to see freedom, as the northern kingdom was exiled before Judah to Assyria in 722 BC because she was also unfaithful to the LORD her God. The year 605 BC began the period of time when Israel's sovereignty was stripped from her and she had to do, from this point on, what she was told by her foreign captures. Israel would not do as the LORD had commanded her, so now she would have to do as her enemies commanded her.

Israel's punishment for her iniquity would be a total of 430 years (remember these are lunar years), which commences in the year 605 BC. Israel spent captive seventy lunar years in Babylon, which was prophesied by the prophet Jeremiah, where he says:

> This whole land shall be a desolation, and an astonishment; and these nations shall serve the king of Bavel [Babylon] seventy years.
>
> Jeremiah 25:11

> For thus says the LORD, "After seventy years are accomplished for Bavel [Babylon], I will visit you, and perform my good word toward you, in causing you to return to this place.
>
> Jeremiah 29:10

First, we must minus the seventy years of Babylonian exile from the 430-year punishment, and we have 360 years remaining.

- 430–70 = 360 biblical years remaining

We now use as a starting point the year Israel was officially released from her Babylonian exile, which was 536 BC, a total of seventy lunar years. Remember, the difference between seventy lunar years verses seventy solar years is approximately 367 days, which total approximately one solar year (605–536 BC). We take the 360 lunar years that remain from the 430 years and subtract it from the year 536 BC, and we should come out with the year Israel's punishment for her unfaithfulness should finish, which is approximately 181 BC.

- 536 BC–360 lunar years = approximately 181 BC

How did I come up with 181 BC?
- We take 360 lunar years and multiply it by 360 days, which equals 129,600 days.
- Then we divide 129,600 days into solar years, which equals approximately 355 solar years.
- 536 BC minus 355 solar years equals approximately the year 181 BC.

But Israel was not reestablished as a sovereign nation in 181 BC. At this point in Israel's history, she was being occupied by Greece. Then at the time of the LORD Jesus's birth, Israel was occupied by Rome. So what is going on here? Is the *prophetic word* spoken through Ezekiel wrong? If you think so, give your head a good shake. Not so hard that it falls off of your shoulders but just enough to realize there must be something missing. What we are missing is a provision in the *Law of Moses,* which says: if Israel is unrepentant after God has dealt with her for her disobedience, God would then multiply her punishment by seven. You will find this revelation in Dr. Jeffery's book *Armageddon, Appointment with Destiny* on pages 38–39.[5] Only God could have revealed this important fact to Dr. Jeffery, for this is what I consider to be one more of the *mysteries of the kingdom of heaven.* It has been in the Bible all along, but it took Dr. Jeffery's eyes to see and his ears to ear so he could find and understand this important provision in the Word of God. I am sure the ancient Jews knew this provision, as it is in the Torah, but I do not know how many of the *new creation* knows it is there. Although there can be no doubt in my mind that the apostle Paul knew this provision was there.

THE PROVISION

When we study Leviticus 26:1–13, we see that God tells Israel that if they "walk in my statutes (his laws), and keep my mitzvot (commandments), and do them" (Leviticus 26:3), he will cause them to prosper, and they would have peace in their land. Israel would chase her enemies, and they would defeat them. In verse eight it says what many Christians like to quote, "Five of you shall chase a hundred, and a hundred of you shall chase ten thousand; and your enemies shall fall before you by the sword" (Leviticus 26:8, HNV). But when we look into the rest of Leviticus chapter twenty-six, we see what happens to the contrary. If Israel does not listen to the LORD and keep his commandments and they break their covenant with him, the LORD will then lift his blessing of health and prosperity from them. It says in verse seventeen, "I will set my face against you, and you shall be struck before your enemies: those who hate you shall rule over you; and you shall flee when none pursues you"

(Leviticus 26:17). This is why the northern kingdom (Samaria) was exiled by Neo-Assyria; and the southern kingdom (Judah) was exiled by Neo-Babylon. These nations ruled over Israel and occupied her land, just as the LORD said. Because Israel did not get back to walking in the statutes of the LORD and obey his commandments when released from Babylonian captivity, the provision in the law of Moses, which we will call *multiplication by seven,* then is activated.

This provision of *multiplication by seven* in the Law of Moses can be found four times in Leviticus chapter 26. It says in verses 18, 21, 23–24, and 27–28 that if Israel does not repent of her breaking God's covenant with her, her punishment will then be multiplied by "seven times." In this case, it means that once Israel was released from their captivity to the Babylonians (which then became the Persians) to rebuild the temple in 536 BC, they had an opportunity to then keep their covenant with the LORD. Because they did not keep their covenant with the LORD, the remainder of their punishment from Ezekiel 4:1–6, which was now 360 lunar years, would be multiplied by seven.

From a study in the writings of Ezra, we see that some of the exiles who returned to Israel, including some of the priests and Levites, did not separate themselves from the women of the foreign nations who practiced abominations, and they had children with them. When these men were confronted with their unfaithfulness, there was a time of confession; but Israel never sincerely got back to walking in the laws of the LORD and being faithful to his commandments. Therefore, their covenant with God was still broken.

Because the provision in the Law of Moses of multiplication by seven was now activated, we have to do some more arithmetic to see what we missed. First, we see that there are still 360 lunar years, which fall under this provision. The reason there are only 360 lunar years that are multiplied by seven, and not the full 430 lunar years, is because God made a promise to the people of Judah that she would spend only seventy lunar years in Babylon. So to keep his promise to them, God had to "unconditionally" minus the seventy years from their 430-year punishment. Since God made the promise of only seventy years in Babylon, he could not go and then add the multiplication by seven formulas to their punishment, even though Israel did not keep God's covenant when they left from their exile. If God did add the formula to the seventy years, he would have broken his promise to them of only seventy years. But the remaining 360 lunar years he could multiply by seven without *breaking any promises* he made to the people of Israel.

We now take the remaining 360 lunar years and multiply them by seven, and we get a total of 2,520 lunar years.

- 360 multiply 7 = 2,520 lunar years

There will now be 2,520 lunar years from the time Israel began to leave Babylon in 536 BC until she would be reestablished as a sovereign nation again. Israel could have been reestablished as a sovereign nation in 181 BC if she had only walked in the statutes of the LORD, therefore keeping his covenant, when they left from their exile to Babylon. But they did not, so Israel would have to wait for the provision of multiplication by seven to run its course before they could shake off the bands of foreign nations.

The Provision Completed

Now we have to figure out what the date will be when the multiplication by seven provisions will end on *the solar calendar.* First, we take 2,520 lunar years and multiply it by 360 days, and we get a total of 907,200 days.

- 2,520 lunar years multiply 360 days equals 907,200 days

We now have 907,200 days from the time Israel began to leave her Babylonian exile until the date she will be reestablished as a sovereign nation once again. We need to take this great number of days and convert it into solar years so we can conclude a fixed date. We take 907,200 days, and divide it by 365.24219, and we get 2,483.8 solar years.

- 907,200 divided by 365.24219 equals 2,483.8 solar years.

I know this might seem like too much arithmetic for some people, and I do not want to fail to keep your interest because of it, but to be precise in the prophetic word of God, these calculations are important. We are dealing with end-time events, and it is very important that we know the times we are living in.

Now we take 2,483.8 solar years and add them to the year and month of April, 536 BC, and we get May, 1948 (rebirth year). Remember to minus one year because there is only one year between 1 BC and AD 1. There is no such thing as 0 BC or AD 0. We can do it this way: 1948 - 2483.8 = Negative 535.8; Negative 535.8 -1 = Negative 536.8. In case you have forgotten because of the math, 536 BC was the year Israel was released from their captivity to the Babylonians to rebuild the temple in Jerusalem.

Now we see why Israel was not reestablished as a sovereign nation until 1948. The reason Israel was not reestablished until this specific year is because she had to first complete her time of punishment imposed on her by God for being unfaithful to him and not keeping the covenant that he made with her. Then once her time was finished, God kept his Word, and she became a (reestablished) nation in *one day*. Isaiah prophesied that this would happen:

> Who has heard such a thing? Who has seen such things? Shall a land be born in one day? Shall a nation be brought forth at once? For as soon as Tziyon [Zion] travailed, she brought forth her children.
>
> Isaiah 66:8

Some people see this prophecy, given through Isaiah, in relation with Israel being released from their Babylonian exile in 536 BC. But this can't be because Israel was not reestablished as a sovereign nation at that time. Israel was still governed in 536 BC by the Persians. Even though she was allowed to go back to the land, it was occupied by the Persians, then the Greeks, then the Romans, and so on.

It was only on May 14, 1948, that Israel was declared a state by Mr. David Ben-Gurion, leader of the Independent Jewish Agency, who administered Jewish affairs in Palestine and the 1947 United Nations Partition Plan Agreement, which gave Israel the right to form a state. The sitting president of the United States, Harry S. Truman, and the Russian leader of the Soviets, Joseph Stalin, recognized Israel as a state right away. Of course, Israel did suffer opposition leading up to this date and also afterwards, by Arab resistance and, sad to say, the British government. But even though the Jews suffered so much resistance, they kept control of their blessed Holy Land only because their time of punishment *was complete.* The remaining 360 lunar years multiplied by seven that was imposed on Israel by the decree of God because of their refusal to sincerely repent and keep the covenant of God came to an end.

It's Hard to Argue

It is hard to dispute the facts and figures that I have brought forth here. Let us say I am not completely accurate with my dates and figures. I believe I am correct, but let's say I am off just a little. Considering how many years we have to deal with here, I could only be off by a year or two. But would anyone dispute the fact Israel was reestablished on May 14, 1948? The whole point is to show how accurate God is in his Word pertaining to his beloved nation of Israel.

Remember what we discussed in chapter four (*The Fig Tree Teaches a Parable*) about Israel being the fig tree in Matthew chapter twenty-four:

> Now from the fig tree learn this parable. When its branch has now become tender, and puts forth its leaves, you know that the summer is near. Even so you also, when you see all these things, know that it is near, even at the doors. Most assuredly I tell you, this generation will not pass away, until all these things are accomplished.
>
> Matthew 24:32–34

Some of the people who witnessed the rebirth of Israel in May of 1948 will still be alive to witness the catching away, the rise of the Antichrist, the seven-year tribulation period, and the second coming of the LORD, Jesus Christ.

The purpose of the information I have shared with you in this chapter was to show how accurate God's Word is. Not only to show that when he predicts an event it happens with pinpoint accuracy, but also to reveal why Israel could not become a nation again until 1948. We must keep in mind that having knowledge of the nation of Israel, especially her rebirth, is important to knowing the season of Christ's return to redeem her. Also, when we have the knowledge of Christ's return for Israel, then we have knowledge of the season when he will come to catch away the church. If the LORD kept his promise to Israel that she would be reborn in a day (see Isaiah 66:8), then he is surely able to keep his promise that the same people who saw her reborn will also see her redeemed.

WHAT IS THE SIGN?

Now that we are beginning to see a little more clearly through the "prophetic word" concerning the nation of Israel that the second coming of Israel's Messiah King is right before us, we must understand that the day and the hour of our LORD's return for the body of Christ is even closer than that. I have shown how accurate the prophetic word has been concerning the first coming of Israel's Messiah King in chapter five (*Daniel's Vision*). Again, we read what it says in Daniel chapter nine:

> Know therefore and discern, that from the going forth of the mitzvah [commandment] to restore and to build Yerushalayim [Jerusalem] to the Messiah the prince, shall be seven weeks, and sixty-two weeks.
>
> Daniel 9:25ab

> After the sixty-two weeks the Anointed One shall be cut off, and shall have nothing.
>
> Daniel 9:26a

This prophetic word given by Gabriel to Daniel was right to the day. The day the decree was given by the Persian king to restore and build Jerusalem, to the day Jesus was rejected by Israel's political and religious leaders total the full sixty-nine-week period. As a reminder, the sixty-nine-week period was *prophetic language* for sixty-nine lunar years multiplied by seven, which equals 483 lunar years. If the total number of prophesied years that Gabriel gave Daniel to record were not fulfilled to the exact number, then we could say it was a false prophetic word. But the total number of years was fulfilled to the exact number to the day because God is always fully accurate whenever he says anything.

In the previous chapter, we saw how accurate God's Word was when he pronounced punishment upon the house of Israel for her unfaithfulness to him. The punishment consisted of a specific number of years multiplied by seven, because a true heart of repentance was ignored, and they continued to not keep God's covenant. God expected Israel to keep their end of the covenant because he would keep his end of it. A covenant works two ways. If one party does not keep their end of the covenant, then the covenant is broken, unless it is an unconditional covenant. But with a conditional covenant (which is what it was), both parties have to keep their end of the covenant for the benefits of the covenant to work.

So as a result of breaking the covenant, Israel fell under the rule of foreign nations until her time of punishment was complete. We saw through the Word of God and through the facts and figures presented that this punishment would not end until May, 1948, which it did, and Israel was reestablished as an independent nation once again. Israel had not been an independent nation since the house of Judah was taken into exile in 605 BC. On May 14, 1948, Israel once again became a sovereign nation, having no foreign nations ruling over her internally or occupying the land she received as an inheritance from the LORD.

Now the land Israel possesses today is not quite all the land the LORD gave to her as an inheritance, but after Israel anoints the Most Holy at the end of her seventieth week, she will regain it all. I also want to add that, unfortunately, there are some powerful nations and a number of groups of people who want to take away from Israel some, and even all, the land she rightly possesses now. But then again, this also is prophesied in the Word of God. I encourage Israel to hold on, because God never breaks his promises!

GOD'S WORD IS ALWAYS ACCURATE

God's prophetic word is accurate. In fact, everything he has given us in the Scriptures is complete and total truth. If what we *think* we know and have is truth, but it does not line up with the truth in the Bible, then we have the wrong truth. The translation of the Bible we study from may have some inaccuracies, but every word God breathed through the writers of the Bible is complete and total truth. If the translation of the Bible we read is off from the original documents, then it's up to us to know where our translation has missed it and learn what the Spirit has really said. Most times it is not what has been translated, but it is the interpretation of that translation.

One of the primary reasons is that not enough study has gone into interpreting the Word and finding out what the Holy Spirit is actually saying. Many teachers will use their denominational doctrines as a foundation to their interpretation instead of the true intent of the Spirit. It is so important to interpret the Word of God properly. Too many times it is not interpreted properly, and the false interpretation leads many astray. Who will give an account for this? Will it be the teacher or the preacher or the hearer? I tend to believe all will be held responsible. The

Holy Spirit will lead those who belong to Jesus into all truth, and he does reveal to us more than just who the Son of God is, you know.

THE DISCIPLES' QUESTIONS

Let us take a look at what Jesus is saying to his disciples on the Mount of Olives when they asked him this question: "Tell us, when these things will be? What is the sign of your coming and of the end of the age?" (Matthew 24:3). Chapter twenty-four of Matthew is known as the *Mount Olive Discourse* and is very important to Israel's future as prophesied in Daniel 9:24–27. Matthew 24:4–35 is a prophetic word taught by Jesus of events that will unfold in Israel's future. We notice in the disciple's question to Jesus they were looking for the answer to three separate events, which were:

A. When these things will be?

B. What is the sign of your coming?

C. The end of the age.

The first question is easy enough, because it refers to the statement Jesus made in verse two, which reads, "Most assuredly I tell you, there will not be left here one stone on another that will not be thrown down" (Matthew 24:2). The LORD was making reference to what will happen to the temple and its buildings when Rome massacred Jerusalem in AD 70.

Now here is an example of making sure we have an accurate translation of the Word of God. In the translation I am using in this book, we can be mistaken by the wording of verse three. In this particular translation, it leads us to believe the disciples are asking when questions B and C will happen. The reason it does this is because it has left out the word *and*. But in the original, which many translations did not omit, the word *and* is inserted in its proper place between the first and second questions. So literally it should read, "Tell us, when shall these be? And what [is] the sign of thy presence [coming], and of the full end of the age?" (Matthew 24:3, Young's Literal Translation). Therefore, literally the disciples are asking Jesus *when the temple will be destroyed*, which relates to question A ("Tell us, when these things will be?") and not when his coming will be, although in question B the disciples do ask Jesus for a "sign" when his "coming" will be. So to repeat, the disciples are literally asking "when" the temple will be destroyed, and they want a "sign" so they can know when his "coming" will take place. Can you see where it could be misleading when we do not have the original intended thought of the writer? It leads to error if one does not properly interpret their particular translation of the Bible. A good Bible teacher would pick up on this and then teach the church accordingly.

The next two questions (B and C) that the disciples asked also take a little insight into what they were actually asking. Whether the disciples actually knew what they were asking, we cannot be sure. What I mean is, they were asking Jesus one thing, but Jesus gave them an answer to another thing. We see in the Gospel of Mark that these actual disciples who asked Jesus this question were Peter, James, John, and Andrew. For them to pose a couple of questions to Jesus like this they all had to be thinking the same thing. Likely, when they were alone at some point away from Jesus, they discussed these two questions amongst themselves, so they likely thought, *Now would be a good time to bring them up*, since Jesus had just initiated their questions with his prophetic statement concerning the temple.

DID THEY KNOW WHAT THEY WERE ASKING?

I have heard somewhere, although I cannot remember where, that the intent of disciples' questions were when Jesus would come and overthrow the occupying forces of their land. Is this what the disciples really had on their mind? It likely was, considering not more then *two months after* they asked Jesus this question, they asked him another question pertaining to the same thought on the same Mount of Olives. They asked Jesus this in the Book of Acts: "Therefore, when they had come together, they asked him, 'LORD, are you now restoring the kingdom to Yisra'el [Israel]?'" (Acts 1:6). But we see this is not the question of thought, which Jesus gave an answer to in Matthew chapter twenty-four. Peter, James, John, and Andrew asked Jesus what they thought was one thing, and he gave them an answer to something completely different.

Answers to both these questions, as I said, take some insight into what Jesus is really saying. Now for most of you who are reading this book, you are likely saying to yourself, "I know what Jesus is saying here!" If this is what you just said to yourself, then I say, "Good. You have the mind of Christ. If you have the mind of Christ, insight into what God is saying will come more easily to you." All believers have the mind of Christ; unfortunately, though, not all are appropriating his mind into their study habits.

WE CAN KNOW!

If you belong to Jesus Christ then never say things like, "Who can know what the LORD is thinking?" or "Who can know the will of the LORD?" If you belong to him, then you should know his thoughts and his will. Some have misinterpreted what Paul said in 1 Corinthians: "For who among men knows the things of a man, except the spirit of the man, which is in him?

Even so, no one knows the things of God, except God's Spirit" (1Corinthians 2:11). Some will say, "See? No one knows the things of God except God's Spirit." Okay, if that is what you believe, or rather, have been taught, then I will retort with, "Is God's Spirit not in you? Is the Spirit not one with your spirit? Does God's Spirit not communicate with your spirit? He is supposed to if you belong to Jesus Christ."

If we take the time to study 1 Corinthians 2:6–16 we will see that Paul is not saying that we *cannot know* what God is saying or thinking. Oh, he *is* to the man who does not have the Spirit of God. But to the man or woman who has the Spirit of God, we *can* know what God is saying, and quite clearly, I will add. And what God is saying is what he is thinking as he communicates his will to us. First Corinthians chapter two says, "Which things also we speak, not in words which man's wisdom teaches, but which the Ruach HaKodesh [Holy Spirit] teaches, comparing spiritual things with spiritual things" (1 Corinthians 2:13). The apostle Paul also adds by the inspiration of the Holy Spirit in verse sixteen: "For who has known the mind of the LORD, that he should instruct him? But we have Messiah's [Christ's] mind" (1 Corinthians 2:16).

Now before some of you want to jump out of your chair and start pulling out your hair, please just wait. Of course, we do not have the same intellect as God the Father. He knows things we will not know until we receive our spiritual bodies, and then he will be able to teach us unfathomable things that we cannot comprehend in these bodies of flesh. But if it is in the Bible, then we can know it now, because the Holy Spirit will teach us. If it is in the Scriptures, you can know clearly what God is saying. Of course, it will take some sincere study, but you can know.

THE KEY

The overall subject of this book is the fact that, as the title says, *the day and the hour is sooner than we think.* All we have discussed pertaining to Israel has to do overwhelmingly with this subject, which relates to the coming of the LORD. The nation of Israel is the key to the LORD's return, both for his second coming and the catching away of the body of Christ. The last two questions of Matthew 24:3, which Jesus answered for Peter and the disciples, have to do with this subject. Again, the disciples asked in the latter portion of this verse, "What is the sign of your coming, and of the end of the age?" (Matthew 24:3b). This may sound like one question, but it is actually two questions in one. That is why I think the disciples did not know what they were actually asking the LORD.

I tend to believe this was the work of the Holy Spirit working through the disciples' question to get Jesus to give our generation some preparation material. By this, I mean some preparatory information concerning the LORD's second coming and the end of the church age. Jesus made the answer very clear to those who have the mind of Christ and are able to discern and interpret his word properly. So let us see what Jesus had to say in response to the disciples' question.

WHERE WAS HIS ANSWER?

Are you wondering, like any inquisitive student of the Bible would, *What happened to part A of the disciple's question, "When these things will be"?* (Matthew 24:3). This was in response to the prophetic word Jesus gave in verse two when he said, "There will not be left here one stone on another, which will not be thrown down." (Matthew 24:2). Jesus never does give Peter and the disciples the time of this event, likely because it was not for them to know at the time of asking, although some of the apostles were still alive when this event took place in AD 70.

This was a horrific time in Israel's history when Ancient Rome totally destroyed the temple and Jerusalem, killing millions of Jews. The other two parts of the disciple's question, 'B' and 'C,' Jesus wants them to have knowledge of, even though all of the disciples would not be alive physically to see the signs take place. But we know the teachings of Jesus were not just for them but for us also, who are living today. Jesus *wants us to know* the answer to these questions likely more than he wanted his disciples to know, because Jesus knew that we, in this generation, would witness the signs of his coming and of the end of the age.

THE NEXT QUESTION

We see the answer Jesus gives in response to the disciple's next question:, "What is the sign of your coming?" (Matthew 24:3b), which was, unbeknownst to them, in reference to the second coming. If you can remember back in chapter four (*The Fig Tree Teaches a Parable*), we actually discussed material that encompasses the answer Jesus gave. We discussed how Jesus's statement in Matthew 24:32 about the fig tree blossoming was unmistakably a reference to the nation of Israel being reestablished. We also mentioned some material about the signs that lead up to the second coming and the catching away. If you like, you can go back and refresh yourself on it, but I will also recapitulate some of the same material as we go along.

Jesus teaches in Matthew 24:4–29 some of the major events that will lead up to his second coming. What I have observed from Scripture is that all these things Jesus lists here, as well those written in the accounts of Mark and Luke, will happen in the seventy-week period. Now, yes, some of these same things are happening even now and have increased intensely over the last half-century—like wars, earthquakes, famines, false prophets appearing, etc. But by and large the list Jesus gives will all be functioning within the tribulation period.

Some people have been taught that either some or all of these events happened in the first century AD, in particular around AD 70. Some of these events that Jesus lists for us may sound like what happened in AD 70, but when we study Revelations, we can see they are fully described in the tribulation period. To prove my point that Jesus was not giving us a list of the events that surrounded the destruction of the temple in AD 70, here is what Jesus says later on in his discourse: "And then the sign of the Son of Man will appear in the sky. Then all the tribes of the eretz [earth] will mourn, and they will see the Son of Man coming on the clouds of the sky with power and great glory" (Matthew 24:30). You are the judge here. Do you think Jesus made an appearance in the sky back then? And did all people of the earth see him coming? The evidence strongly suggests he and they did not.

In Matthew 24:30, Jesus is describing to the disciples the signs preceding his second coming. But Jesus gives them even greater evidence that what he speaks is true with the statement he makes in Matthew 24:32, which is Israel's renewed independence with the parable of the fig tree blossoming. Remember, I said in chapter four that the disciples would have known without any doubt what Jesus was saying with this parable. They knew that this parable of the fig tree represented the nation of Israel, and they knew it meant Israel's independence as a sovereign nation once again. You must understand that the disciples knew, from the prophecies of Daniel and also what it says in Lamentations chapter four, that Israel would receive her independence again. "The punishment of your iniquity is accomplished, daughter of Tziyon [Zion]; he will no more carry you away into captivity: He will visit your iniquity, daughter of Edom; he will uncover your sins" (Lamentations 4:22).

Remember, Israel's punishment for her iniquity ended in May 1948. Peter and the disciples just did not know when this great day for the nation would be. So now the disciples know that *Israel's sovereignty* is related to the LORD's *coming*. Then Jesus makes the time of his coming even more clear to them with this statement in verses thirty-three and thirty-four: "Even so you also, when you see all these things, know that it is near, even at the doors. Most assuredly I tell you, this generation will not pass away, until all these things are accomplished" (Matthew 24:33–34). Peter and the disciples know that the LORD's coming will be before the generation of people who witnessed Israel's reestablishment pass away. This is the sign Jesus gave the disciples to their unrealized question from Matthew 24:3 pertaining to his second coming, which was prophesied in Daniel 9:24.

THE THIRD QUESTION

Now we will look at the last part of the disciples' question, which was, "What will be the sign of … the end of the age?" (Matthew 24:3b). Jesus does not mention this part of their question anywhere between verses four to thirty-five. This phrase refers to *the end of the church age,* which is in reference to the *catching away* of Christ's body. Some people may disagree with me that this phrase has anything to do with the catching away or the end of the church age, but as we begin to study Matthew 24:36–51, it will make more sense. We will do this in the next chapter.

The disciples could not have known what they were asking Jesus at this time, because they had no idea there would even be a church age. The church age did not begin until Jesus died and rose again and made it possible for Jews and Gentiles to become one in Christ. Some believe the church age began the day of Pentecost, when a group of about 120 people were gathered, seeking the LORD, and they were all filled with the Holy Spirit, and the Spirit gave them power to speak in other languages (see Acts 2:1–4). But I see where the church age began before the day of Pentecost. I see it happening the *very first day* Jesus rose from the dead.

When we look at the Gospel of John, we see in chapter twenty that Mary Magdalene, Peter, and John find Jesus's tomb empty on the day Jesus was raised from the dead. We see Jesus came and stood in the midst of where the disciples were assembled, and he said to them: "Shalom [peace] be to you." John 20:19c). Jesus shows them his hands and feet to prove to them it is he they are seeing, and Peter and the disciples were glad to see the LORD. Then we see where Jesus breathed on the disciples and said to them, "Receive the Ruach HaKodesh!" (John 20:22), which means the *Holy Spirit*. This action of Jesus released the person of the Holy Spirit to become one with the spirits of those whom Jesus breathed on. Instantly, these persons were *born again* because they put their faith in Jesus and believed that he was raised from the dead (because they saw him with their own eyes), and they confessed Jesus as LORD. We see in verse twenty-eight where Thomas makes the confession that Jesus is LORD, "Toma [Thomas] answered him, "My LORD and my God!" (John 20:28). This is when the church age officially began—the very first day when the disciples received the Holy Spirit, which was the evening of the first day of Christ's resurrection. On the day of Pentecost, when the fire of the Holy Spirit came upon the group of about 120 people, they were already new creations.

Now there is a day when the church age will officially come to an end, and this is the day that encompasses this question (which the disciples asked), "The end of the age." This day will precede the second coming of the LORD by at least seven years. By seven years, I mean seven lunar years, not seven solar years. When we do the math, there is only a thirty-seven-day difference between the two time periods, giving the solar years the most time, according to the period of days. These thirty-seven days can confuse those who are studying God's Word if they do not interpret the Word correctly. So I think it is better to be as accurate as we can. The church age will end before Israel's seventieth week begins, with the antichrist ratifying a covenant with them to begin this seven-year period.

So we see, Jesus answers the disciples' question for them in pretty good detail. His coming will be before all the people pass away who witnessed Israel reestablished as a sovereign nation in 1948. He also answers their unknowingly asked question, when the church age will end, with the same answer. The church age will be complete between Israel's reestablishment and before the people who witnessed it pass away. This only confirms that *the day and the hour is sooner than we think.*

The Catching Away

I would like to show in this chapter that Jesus taught about the church and her being snatched (taken very quickly) out of this earth in his teaching to Peter and the disciples on the Mount of Olives. I know some in the church have their doubts about this, and they believe Jesus was speaking about Israel only in the whole of Matthew chapter twenty-four and the synoptic gospels that parallel with this chapter. Then there are others in the church who, like me, believe that Jesus taught about the church and its catching away, not only in Matthew chapter twenty-four, but in other passages as well.

I will agree that many of Jesus's parabolic teachings do pertain to Israel only, but not all of them. For example, in Matthew 13:24–30; 37–43 we see Jesus's parable of the weeds that were sown among the wheat. Jesus said, "The kingdom of heaven is like a man who sowed good seed in his field" (Matthew 13:24). He explains in Matthew 13:37–38, that the man who sowed the good seed is the *Son of Man*, which is in reference to himself. The good seed refers to the *sons of the kingdom,* which is in reference to those who put their faith in the Son of Man.

It says in Romans chapter eight, "the Spirit himself testifies with our spirit that we are children of God; and if children, then heirs; heirs of God, and joint-heirs with Messiah [Christ]"

(Romans 8:16–17a). These two verses imply that we are *sons and daughters* of the kingdom. Without going on to explain the rest of this parable in Matthew chapter thirteen, we can see that Jesus is teaching about the sons of the kingdom of heaven, and these sons are those who have made Jesus their Lord, so he was not referring to Israel but the new creation in this particular parable.

We also see in Luke chapter twelve where Jesus tells his disciples in verse twenty-two, "Don't be anxious for your life, what you will eat, nor yet for your body, what you will wear" (Luke 12:22). He goes on to explain to them to seek God's kingdom, and the Father's provision will be with them. In verse thirty-two, Jesus says to them, "Don't be afraid, little flock, for it is your Father's good pleasure to give you the Kingdom" (Luke 12:32). So is Jesus talking to Israel only in this verse? No! Jesus was initially teaching his disciples whom he had chosen to be the first Christians. This passage is also for everyone who is of the household of God being built on the foundation of these same disciples. Do we believers not use this passage of scripture as a principle to live by? Yes, we do most certainly. The point I am trying to make is that Jesus did teach on the Mount of Olives in Matthew chapter twenty-four about the body of Christ (along with the house of Israel) and the catching away.

Jesus Reveals the Catching Away
Jesus has just explained to Peter and the disciples (in Matthew 24:32–34) that his second coming would be witnessed by those who witnessed the rebirth of the nation of Israel. As we have learned, this is the first time Judah has been self-governing since she went into exile to the Babylonians in 605 bc. Israel could not be free from Gentile occupation until her punishment for iniq-

uity was complete, which was in May of 1948. Jesus continues with his teaching to reveal also to the disciples knowledge of the catching away of the church.

Jesus has to teach the disciples of this very important event because, as said, the apostles are the foundation of the church. The apostle Paul writes in Ephesians:

> So then you are no longer strangers and foreigners, but you are fellow citizens with the holy ones [the saints], and of the household of God, being built on the foundation of the Apostles and Prophets, Messiah [Christ] Yeshua [Jesus] himself being the chief cornerstone; in whom the whole building, fitted together, grows into a holy temple in the LORD; in whom you also are built together for a habitation of God in the Spirit.
>
> Ephesians 2:19–22

These men are not only the *foundation stones* of the church, but they will be among those who will be caught up to meet the LORD in the air when that *day and hour* occurs.

TO RECTIFY SOME CONFUSION

Jesus begins with this statement in Matthew chapter twenty-four to speak to the church: "But no one knows of that day and hour, not even the angels of heaven, but my Father only" (Matthew 24:36). Many who believe that Jesus does not speak of the body of Christ or the catching away of the church in this chapter of Matthew's gospel say that this verse is referring to the second coming, but I refute this theory and will explain. Jesus *could not* have been referring to his second coming with this statement, because contrary to what some say, some people *will know* the day of the second coming.

People will be able to know in advance *the exact day* of the second coming, just as Israel's religious leaders *should have known* the day of the Messiah's first arrival. What I mean is, the prophecies with their calculations: were there for them like they are here for you and me. Remember in chapter five (*Daniel's Vision*), when we discussed the prophecy in Daniel 9:25–26, which predicted with total accuracy to the day when Jesus would present himself to Israel as their Messiah King, and then Israel rejected him? The prophecy says that there will be a total of 483 lunar years from the day the decree was given to restore and build Jerusalem to the Messiah's arrival, and then his people will cut him off. This prophecy was *accurate to the day,* as it should be, because God's Word is *always* on the mark. If you want to go back and refresh your mind and spirit with this information, then go ahead, for I am sure it will build you up.

So, if this portion of Daniel's prophecy was correct to the day, then why would there be any flaws in the rest of this prophetic word? Daniel 9:24 says there will be 490 lunar years until Israel anoints Jesus as their Messiah King. As said, this prophetic word was perfect with its prediction that after the first 483 lunar years Israel's Messiah would come, and they would reject him. Now it is clear to see that Israel has only seven lunar years left (from the prophecy in Daniel) until their Messiah comes again, but this time they will receive him.

- 490 lunar years–483 lunar years = 7 lunar years

Daniel's prophecy actually makes it easy for one to calculate *to the day* when Christ will come to Israel the second time.

It says the starting point will be when the antichrist makes a firm covenant with Israel for the last seven lunar years of Israel's decreed 490 lunar year period. If the Word of God is accurate, and I know it is, then there will be precisely 2,520 days, which are seven lunar years exactly from the day Israel agrees to a covenant with the Antichrist, until she anoints her *true* Messiah. So, as I said, people will know the day of the second coming if they have knowledge of this prophecy and can calculate the prophecy correctly. Without doubt there will be people who have missed the catching away and will then partake in Israel's seventieth-week period (tribulation period) who will know to the day when the second coming of the LORD Jesus will be.

THIS KNOWLEDGE IS VITALLY IMPORTANT

There will be multiple millions of people saved in the tribulation period that the LORD will direct this information to so they can know when Jesus will come for them. These people will be looking to that day of the LORD's second coming, unlike the many right now who are not looking to the catching away of the church. The tribulation period will be the most terrible time this world has ever seen, so instinctually the people in it will hasten the return of the LORD. Not all will be martyred by the enemy in the tribulation period, even though millions will be put to death. Many people will come to know the truth, from all nations and cultures, and they will have to live through this horrific time of the tribulation. These will be among those who actually witness the LORD coming in the clouds (see Matthew 24:30–31; Revelation 1:7; Zechariah 12:10–13:1). And they will know, if they do the calculations of Gabriel's prophetic word to Daniel correctly, the exact day when Christ will come to redeem Israel.

So we can see that Jesus was not referring to the day of his second coming but the day of the catching away of the church with this statement: "But no one knows of that day and hour, not even the angels of heaven, but my Father only" (Matthew 24:36). To strengthen my case, I would like to say that there are no specific prophecies that tell us the exact day the catching away of the body of Christ will be. Because Matthew 24:36 is a reference to the catching away and not to the second coming, this knowledge is kept from the angels of heaven and also the Son, as the Gospel of Mark records. Only the Father knows this day. The time the Son will know of the catching away of the church, who is actually the bride, is when his Father sends him to get his beloved. Jesus said to his disciples in John chapter fourteen:

> Don't let your heart be troubled. Believe in God. Believe also in me. In my Father's house are many mansions. If it weren't so, I would have told you. I am going to prepare a place for you. If I go and prepare a place for you, I will come again, and will receive you to myself; that where I am, you may be there also.
>
> John 14:1–3

Does this not sound a lot like an ancient Middle Eastern betrothal? The young woman and her betrothed would be arranged in marriage, and after a certain amount of time the betrothed would go to his bride's house to get her and bring her to his father's house. It is here in his father's house they will live and start a life together.

The End of an Age: The Last Time

Here is some of what we do know about the day and hour of the catching away. To begin with, we know it will happen in the *last time*, which refers to the last time of the church age. The last time of the church age is the *last portion of time* just before the beginning of Israel's seventieth-week period. We do not know if the catching away is one day before, or a week before, or however long before Israel's seventieth-week begins. We know Israel's seventieth week starts with the Antichrist confirming a covenant with the nation of Israel. The Antichrist is the "man of sin, the son of destruction" (2 Thessalonians 2:3 and 8). He is the one in Daniel's prophesy referred to as "the prince who shall come" (Daniel 9:26), and he will not be revealed until the body of Christ and the Holy Spirit's *function as* Comforter to the church are taken out of the way first. You can see this in 2 Thessalonians 2:1–12, where it will benefit you enormously to study this passage.

We see that Peter mentions the catching away will not happen until the last time. In First Peter chapter one it says:

> Blessed be the God and Father of our Lord Yeshua [Jesus] the Messiah [Christ], who according to his great mercy became our father again to a living hope through the resurrection of Yeshua [Jesus] the Messiah [Christ] from the dead, to an incorruptible and undefiled inheritance that doesn't fade away, reserved in heaven for you, who by the power of God are guarded through faith for a salvation ready to be revealed in the last time.
>
> 1 Peter 1:3–5

"The salvation ready to be revealed" (1 Peter 1:5) refers to the *redemption of our individual physical bodies* as the apostle Paul describes in First Corinthians chapter fifteen:

> Behold, I tell you a mystery. We will not all sleep, but we will all be changed, in a moment, in the twinkling of an eye, at the last shofar [trumpet]. For the shofar [trumpet] will sound, and the dead will be raised incorruptible, and we will be changed.
>
> 1 Corinthians 15:51–52

THE LAST DAYS

The catching away of the body of Christ will be in the last days of the generation of people who witnessed the reestablishment of the nation of Israel before they all pass away. The apostle Peter writes again about the catching away of the body of Christ when he writes in Second Peter chapter three:

> In the last days mockers will come, walking after their own lusts, and saying, "Where is the promise of his coming? For, from the day that the fathers fell asleep, all things continue as they were from the beginning of the creation.
>
> 2 Peter 3:3–4

The promise of his coming refers to the catching away of the church, not the second coming. The promise pertains to the promise the LORD Jesus made in John 14:1–3 to his disciples and all those who believe in him, as we have just read. Again, Jesus said in verse three of that passage, "If I go and prepare a place for you, I will come again, and will receive you to myself; that where

I am, you may be there also" (John 14:3). This statement sounds like a promise to me that I know Jesus will keep!

Peter is addressing Christians in his letter—those who are part of the new covenant. Christians are *caught up* in the catching away, so why would we be looking for the second coming? The second coming is primarily to redeem and rescue Israel and the tribulation saints from the destruction of the Antichrist and his armies, and most importantly to *bring an end* to Israel's iniquities. Peter's initial readers were looking forward to the return of the LORD, first and foremost so their physical bodies could be redeemed and their salvation completed. Like I said, this promise is one Jesus will keep, but there will be those who mock the words of Jesus in the last days. Sad to say, these mockers will primarily be those who go to church.

SO NEAR!

We also know that the catching away is near, for this is what the half brother of Jesus wrote:

> Be patient therefore, brothers, until the coming of the LORD. Behold, the farmer waits for the precious fruit of the eretz [earth], being patient over it, until it receives the early and late rain. You also be patient. Establish your hearts, for the coming of the LORD is at hand.
>
> James 5:7–8

James addresses his readers as "brothers," which means he is writing to those who are believers in the LORD. James wrote this epistle anywhere from fifteen to thirty years *after* Jesus ascended into heaven. If James said the coming of the LORD was near back in the first century then how near can it be now? (Especially with what we now know about Israel).

ONLY LOGICAL

Jesus continues his teaching to the disciples about his coming for the church, and he uses the similarity of it being like in the days of Noah. The LORD Jesus says:

> As the days of Noach [Noah] were, so will be the coming of the Son of Man. For as in those days which were before the flood they were eating and drinking, marrying and giving in marriage, until the day that Noach [Noah] entered into the teivah [ark].
>
> Matthew 24:37–38

Jesus is saying that when he comes for his church, people will be carrying on with everyday life as usual, just as it was in Noah's day. People were eating, drinking, and getting married as if everything would be like this today and the next day and forever. But when it comes to the end of Israel's seventieth-week period, it is hard to see people carrying on with *the everyday way* of life, especially the very day the LORD comes to rescue Israel and the tribulation saints.

When we read the revelation of Jesus to John, we see that there will be *great catastrophe* on the earth the very day of the second coming. When Jesus comes for Israel the second time the battle of Armageddon will be raging, so I don't think people will be just living life as they do today, eating and drinking, marrying, and giving in marriage. This statement Jesus makes in Matthew 24:37–38 is inconsistent with what will be taking place on the earth at the second coming. So it has to mean that when here he uses the phrase, "So will be the coming of the Son of Man" (Matthew 24:37), Jesus is referring to the catching away of the church. Jesus goes on to say, "And they didn't know until the flood came and took them all away, so will be the coming of the Son of Man" (Matthew 24:39). Noah's contemporaries had no idea that this rain that was falling from the sky would be enough to cause a flood and take them all away. The flood caught the people by surprise. Likewise, when the LORD comes and *captures away* the body of Christ, many people will be in total shock.

The LORD continues: "Then two men will be in the field: one will be taken and one will be left; two women grinding at the mill, one will be taken and one will be left" (Matthew 24:40–41). Remember, Jesus makes this statement within the context of the catching away, when people will be living their daily routine of eating, drinking, and getting married. Then in 24:40–41 he refers to them at their place of employment, where they make their living. To reiterate my point, can people be at their place of work toiling to make a living, just living life as it comes to them, when the battle of Armageddon is taking place? No, they cannot, unless they are androids! This passage is in the context of the catching away, where people will be at their place of employment, and they will have no idea what is about to transpire over the entire earth. Those who belong to Jesus Christ will be *snatched away* from the earth, and those who do not belong to him will be left to enter into the final seven years of Israel's iniquity.

I believe that we are seeing in this portion of Jesus's teaching, starting at verse thirty-six, that Jesus is describing to the disciples the catching away instead of his second coming. Now I would like to show Christ's position pertaining to a state of readiness of the catching away. But we will do this in the next chapter.

THE FAITHFUL AND
WISE SERVANT

As we learned in the previous chapter, Jesus did teach his disciples about the catching away of the church. He teaches them that when this day comes, people will be carrying on with everyday living just as they always have. People will be eating and drinking, rising out of bed, and going to work to earn a living as people do repetitiously day after day. Many couples will even have their wedding day scheduled on this day.

Can you imagine the excitement of the people who are getting married on this day waking up on this very special morning and expecting to have the greatest day of their life and then suddenly millions of people vanish all over the world? What will the bridegroom do if his best man ends up being one of the faithful ones who end up missing (and he has the ring)? What about the bride, who I am sure is a bundle of nerves already, has her bridesmaid not show up to help her get ready? This day will be like nothing the world has every seen up to this point. How many Christians will also have their wedding scheduled for this day? They will, you know, because no one knows the day and the hour of the coming of the LORD.

The day of the catching away will certainly be like in the days of Noah, when Noah's contemporaries had no idea until that day the immediate change that was coming upon their lives. In their case, the flood came and took them all away to their death. Even Noah and his family did not know the exact day when the LORD would flood the earth. All they knew was that it was coming, and they had to have the ark prepared and themselves ready and in the ark. For the people who are not part of the catching away, their lives will have an immediate change when worldwide panic hits because of the sudden disappearance of what I assume will be hundreds of millions of people. Can you imagine the fear that will fill the earth on this day? At least, I assume this will be the emotional state of most people, because I do not see in the Bible any record of the people's reaction to the disappearance of multiple millions of people all over the world at once.

THERE ARE EXPECTATIONS

As we continue to study Matthew's text, we learn that Jesus has expectations for those of us who belong to him in particular to the day and the hour of the catching away. Jesus's position is firm that we be *watching and ready* for him on that day. Some people likely wonder how we can be watching and ready for him when we do not even know the day and the hour of his coming for us. If you have ever thought this, you are not alone. But your answer is in your question. The fact we do not know the day and the hour is *precisely* the reason why we should be *watching* so we can be *ready* for the catching away. An athlete does not lie on his couch eating potato chips and drinking colas all day long, waiting for the greatest event of his life to happen. If he does, he will never make it across the finish line. The athlete's coach and personal trainer know this much, which is why they persistently drill into his mind and his actions to watch himself and be ready for his big event. We who belong to the LORD are like athletes. We need to be watching and be ready for the *greatest upcoming event* of our born-again lives.

Jesus makes this stern demand to his disciples and all those who will come after them when he says, "Watch therefore, for you don't know in what hour your LORD comes" (Matthew 24:42). The demand is to be watching, and I say it is a stern demand because Jesus does not want his disciples *to be moved off of* or *to stop obeying* this demand. Jesus is demanding that his disciples be unrelenting in their effort to watch for the hour when the LORD will come. In other words, Jesus wants all who belong to him to watch for his appearing with zeal. We can almost say that this phrase is a command by how much it demands our attention. We cannot ignore the commands of the LORD.

Why would Jesus demand that we watch for this hour of his coming? Can you see how Jesus worded this phrase? He did not speak in 24:42 like he spoke in Matthew 24:36, when he said to watch the day and hour. "But no one knows of that day and hour." No, he did not. But in Matthew 24:42, Jesus only uses the word *hour* instead of the *day and hour*. The likely reason Jesus is specific with his wording here is because of his demand to watch. Jesus wants those of us who belong to him to be watching *up to the very minute* for the catching away of the church. He does not want us to be slack in this demand, which is really a command, as Christ knows all so well that many will neglect this command.

ARE YOU NEGLIGENT?
How many Christians are watching *right now* for the LORD to come and take up quickly the body of Christ? We know for sure that those who do not have the seal of God's ownership on

them are not watching for Jesus to come. They are not watching because they have no knowledge of this event, so how can they be watching? Although there are some unbelievers whom I have witnessed to and have shared this event with, and they believe this event is true, the Word has not yet had a chance to grow in them, and they do not take the message of the catching away seriously. But what about believers? How many believers do you think are "watching for the day" of the glorious appearing of our Lord? How many believers do you think are even prepared to be watching right up to the very hour of his return? Jesus wants us to be watching for his return right up to the very hour of it, or he would not make the demand to "watch therefore." Right now is a good time to begin to watch (and be ready) for the catching away, especially with the knowledge we have that Christ's second coming is right at the door. Watching for the coming of the Lord means to pay attention to the signs he gives in his word that will take place in the world prior to this event. For example, Israel's rebirth is the primary sign that this is the generation of his coming, so the Christian rather than living like Christ's coming is two hundred years from now, should be watching for his coming now. Watching not only means to pay attention to the signs, but it also means to be anticipating Christ's return in your heart, rather than being indifferent to his return. We need to watch with our heart.

BE DILIGENT

Jesus continues with his teaching, and says this:

> But know this, that if the master of the house had known in what watch of the night the thief was coming, he would

have watched, and would not have allowed his house to be broken into.

Matthew 24:43

Because Jesus begins this illustration with the phrase "but know this" suggests he is emphatic that those who are listening *understand completely* what it is he is saying. The illustration is of a thief who has (and the emphasis is on the word *has*) broken into a man's house. Now the master of the house does not represent anyone in particular, only that he is the one who *had* his house broken into. If the man would have had even the slightest hint of what time the thief was coming, he would have *stood guard* and not allowed his house to be burglarized.

This illustration would have made perfect sense to the disciples. They likely thought amongst themselves, *If only any man could have the knowledge that a thief was coming, then he would watch for him even if it takes all night so he can be ready for when the thief arrives.* Breaking into one's house was a good way to get the disciples attention, because nobody wants their house broken into. Every wise man would take every precaution to guard and protect not only his house and property but especially his wife and children who are inside.

BE READY

Jesus makes the parallel to this illustration in the next verse. Jesus says, "Therefore also be ready, for in an hour that you don't expect, the Son of Man will come" (Matthew 24:44). Again, Jesus is keeping within the context of his demand to be alert as he repeats the phrase "in an hour." Just like a man would be watching for a thief if he has knowledge of him coming, so we too must be watching so we can be ready for the hour of the catching away. The man in this illustration did not know the hour the thief was coming to break into his house, as we do not know the hour the LORD will come. The man did not expect his house to be broken into, or he would have been watching for the thief so he could be ready to subdue him. The point of Jesus's illustration is that *if the man knew* the thief was coming, he would *get prepared* for him.

Jesus says he is coming for the church in an hour we do not expect him to come, but even so, we are still supposed to be ready for him. He would not demand we be ready for him if we could not be. We already have a great deal of knowledge of his coming for the church. Review the material we have been discussing in this book. We have already learned that the second coming of the LORD to redeem Israel and put away her iniquity is only a few short years away from this year 2010. If the people who saw (more precisely, were able to comprehend) Israel reestablished in 1948 live to at least the statistical life expectancy of seventy-nine to eighty years, then they have the potential (if they live long enough and were not redeemed at the catching away of the church) to see Christ at his second coming. The problem is, only someone who has no intention of watching for the LORD to come to catch away his bride will try to downplay that this event is near. Only those who are wise will take Jesus at his Word to watch so they can be ready "for you don't know in what hour your LORD comes" (Matthew 24:42).

SOME ACT CARELESS

Some Christians carelessly fling this following statement around with such pride in their boast as they say, "I am ready to meet the LORD anytime." But all the while, some of these do not wish the bridegroom to come anytime soon, especially not in their lifetime. Their desire is not to see the plan of the Father come to pass, because his plan does not fit in with their life's agenda, so they think. The most frequent excuse some use to hide their secret desire is that there are so many more people to be saved. But usually some of these same people do not do much to get anyone saved. Yes, we should be preaching and teaching the Word of God daily so people can have the opportunity to receive it, right up to the very day and hour. But the hour of the LORD's return is going to come with billions of people who are still not saved. Nonetheless, the Son of Man expects us to be watching so we can be ready for the catching away. The catching away of the church is in the plan of the Father, and it has been from the start. That is why the infant church was looking for the LORD's coming when they were alive. It has been more then 1,970 years since Paul began to introduce the idea of the catching away, and we are still waiting for the LORD to snatch us up. But as I have discussed already, some other important facts had to be established first, like the reestablishment of Israel. Starting in chapter ten, we will look at the warning Jesus gives the church about being ready through the parable of the ten virgins, but first we will look at what Jesus has to say to those who are leaders in the church concerning the day and the hour.

UNDERSTANDING: AGAIN

In the rest of Matthew chapter twenty-four, starting with verse forty-five, we see Jesus has placed a great deal of responsibility on those whom he has put in charge over the church. Jesus continues to speak in parables, using symbolic language. Can you remember from chapter one (*Why Parables?*) why Jesus spoke in parabolic language to the people? I also made mention of it in chapter two. Jesus often spoke to the people in parables because he says, "To you it is given to know the mysteries of the Kingdom of Heaven, but it is not given to them" (Matthew 13:11). In other words, Christ's parabolic teachings are mysteries of the Father's Kingdom, which are not comprehendible to those who are outside of the household of God. Jesus said to his disciples, "Therefore, I speak to them in parables, because seeing they don't see, and hearing, they don't hear, neither do they understand" (Matthew 13:13). When we study Matthew chapter thirteen, we see that Jesus would speak in parables when he taught the crowds, but when he was alone with the disciples he would reveal the parables to them so they could understand.

Some theologians, some scholars, and some lay people have read and studied God's Word, but the mysteries of the kingdom they cannot understand because they are outside of the household of God. Then there are some, who are of the household of God, who cannot understand the mysteries because for various reasons they are not listening to the Spirit of God as he is revealing. The disciples whom Jesus initially taught his parables to were of the household of God, so they had ears to hear and understand what he was teaching after Jesus took them aside to reveal the mysteries to them. They were listening as God was revealing. God has preserved his Word for us in this generation through all the various translations that we have today. Even today, like in the first century, those who are of the kingdom and have eyes to see and ears to hear still need Jesus through the Spirit to teach us the mysteries of the kingdom of heaven.

We see in verse forty-five, Jesus says, "Who then is the faithful and wise servant, whom his LORD has set over his household, to give them their food in due season?" (Matthew 24:45). What is Jesus teaching with this statement? This verse, along with the rest of this passage in Matthew 24:45–51, is symbolic language Jesus used that is *exclusively* for the household of God, meaning it is for those who have eyes to see and ears to hear. It is for those who hear the Word and understand what Jesus is saying. Much of the New Testament is in straightforward language, but we still need the Spirit to help us understand what he is really saying. But with the teachings of Jesus in the gospel records, his teachings take some extra digging into, because Christ's teaching style was with parables. But because we have eyes to see and ears to hear, we can, with the help of the Holy Spirit, understand what the LORD is saying to us. This is why when God is revealing, we should be listening.

People can read this passage in Matthew 24:45–51 and come up with many differing opinions to what Jesus is saying, but he is saying only one thing, and he is using symbolic language to say it. Look at the context in which this passage is taught. Jesus taught this within the context of his second coming and the catching away of the church. Having this knowledge, with the help of the Spirit, we should be able to see and hear what Jesus was initially teaching to Peter, John, James, Andrew, and now you and me. In this passage, Jesus is teaching about those whom he has appointed to his kingdom offices and the responsibilities he has given them in the *generation* of the second coming and the catching away.

KINGDOM OFFICERS: AGENTS OF THE KINGDOM

Being confident that we can understand what Jesus is teaching, let us look at the symbolism Jesus uses in Matthew 24:45: To begin with, "his LORD" refers to God; being more specific, it refers to Jesus. The Webster Bible, which is a translation by Noah Webster in 1833, translates LORD with a capital letter, therefore reading LORD. Some versions of the Bible may have translated LORD as *master*. Next, "The faithful and wise servant" (Matthew 24:45a) is symbolic of the kingdom office people (appointees), whom the LORD has called. It says in Ephesians chapter four,

> He gave some to be apostles; and some, prophets; and some, evangelists; and some, shepherds and teachers; for the perfecting of the holy ones, to the work of serving, to the building up of the body of Messiah; until we all attain to the unity of the faith, and of the knowledge of the Son of God, to a full grown man, to the measure of the stature of the fullness of Messiah.
>
> Ephesians 4:11–13

Do you notice that in Matthew's text, Jesus said that it was he (symbolically speaking) who set this group of kingdom office people (appointees) over his household? The Greek word Matthew used for "set over" has the connotation of one being appointed with authority to minister in an office capacity. In other words, "the faithful and wise servant" (Matthew 24:45a) has been *appointed* with a special duty. We continue with "His household," which refers to God's people, namely the body of Christ. It says in Ephesians chapter two, "So then you are no longer strangers and foreigners, but you are fellow citizens with the holy ones, and of the household of God" (Ephesians 2:19). After that we have "their food," which refers to the Word of God, especially the *mysteries* of the kingdom of heaven (see Matthew 13:11). Then finally, "In due season" (Matthew 24:45c) refers to the right season of time. Matthew used the Greek word *kai-*

ros, which, according to Young's Analytical Concordance, means "certain season; or convenient season; or due season."[6]

- His LORD: Jesus
- The faithful and wise servant: Kingdom Office appointees
- His household: The church
- Their food: The Word of God (especially the mysteries)
- In due season: The right season of time

So those appointed to the kingdom offices—the apostles, prophets, evangelists, pastors and teachers—are to teach the body of Christ the Word, especially giving them help to understand the mysteries of the kingdom. The second coming and the catching away of the church are mysteries, or hidden things, of the kingdom of heaven. They are mysteries because it takes *spiritual insight* to know and understand the full scope of these teachings.

HOW MUCH DO WE KNOW?

If we were to interview people outside of the household of God, they likely would have absolutely zero knowledge on these teachings. Perhaps I should not be as dogmatic, as some of this group might have a slight knowledge of the second coming and of the catching away. Now, if we were to interview most Christians on these subjects, how much knowledge of these teachings do we have? My observation is that many in the household of God have nowhere near the knowledge of these teachings as we should have. If we do not have the proper amount of knowledge of the second coming and of the catching away like we are supposed to, then how can we watch and be ready (like we are commanded) for the day when our redemption is made complete?

The reason I can express such a strong opinion against the house of God not having sufficient teaching about the catching away is because so many Christians give all kinds of excuses why the second coming and the catching away cannot happen while they are still in their physical body. This tells me that they have no knowledge of the basic teaching pertaining to the timing of these two events, which we have discussed in this book. I dare not put all Christians in the same category, because there are some who do have insight into the second coming and the catching away, and they are watching and getting prepared as the LORD has commanded. But the whole body of Christ must have this revelation because *we are all one* in Christ. Having such a divide in this important revelation is like a head that has no eyes or no ears. Because the head lacks eyes and ears it then cannot see or hear.

WHAT ARE WE EATING?

Why does the house of God have little to no knowledge of the second coming and of the catching away and, especially, of their timing? There are a number of reasons, but the number-one reason is that the church is not being properly fed the knowledge. The faithful and wise servants (those appointed to these positions of spiritual authority) are to teach the mysteries of the kingdom in the right season. The right season to teach the second coming and of the catching away of the church is most certainly in the generation that these events will occur. As we have been learning, with the reestablishment of Israel as being our primary time clock, this is the due season. The faithful and wise servants are to teach the household of God on these subjects so the house can "watch therefore" and to "be ready," because we do not know the hour our LORD will come for us. If the household of God is fed their food in its due season, then we would know at least the approximate time of the second coming and therefore have an intelligent idea of when the catching away will occur.

We Must Have the Proper Diet: At the Right Time

The LORD follows up the *Kingdom Office Manual* (this is what I call Matthew 24:45) on which food to be feeding the household (and when) with an incentive in Matthew 24:46 to the faithful and wise servants to follow his instructions. Jesus says, "Blessed is that servant whom his LORD finds doing so when he comes" (Matthew 24:46). The LORD has just inferred that those called to kingdom office positions *are blessed* if they are *found feeding the household* of God the *proper food* when he comes. The connotation of the word *blessed,* in this verse, has more to do with receiving something than it does with being happy. Although if the servant does what the LORD tells him to, namely giving the household their proper food in due season, he would not be happier.

The pastor and teacher, along with the apostles, prophets, and evangelists, must be teaching the church as much as they can, to the extent of their knowledge, biblical information of the LORD's coming. *It is the season to be doing so!* Teaching the church these things will help the church to be watching so we can be ready. If those appointed to kingdom office positions have no knowledge on the second coming and the catching away of the church, then it is up to them to get the knowledge. What excuse will the teacher of the Word give if they have not prepared the body of Christ for the hour when the Son of Man comes?

Preparations start with at least *not denying* that the second coming is almost at the door and the catching away even closer then that. If anyone holds a kingdom office position and does not believe this, then may I lovingly suggest that you open your eyes so you can see and unblock your ears and hear what the LORD is really saying? You should be the one sitting so you can be taught and allow the LORD to bring in another appointee so the body of Christ can be *taught* and *instructed* on how to get ready for her greatest day since our salvation began. You need to be listening while the LORD is revealing! The teaching of the LORD's coming, both his second coming and the catching away is the primary message of this generation, along with the message of salvation, of course (the two messages are interlaced in this generation). We cannot neglect the rest of the Word of God either, because it is part of the diet of preparation.

WHAT AN INCENTIVE!

As said, there will be *great compensation* to those who teach the church to be watching and to be ready for the coming of the LORD. The LORD says in verse forty-seven, "Most assuredly I tell you that he will set him over all that he has" (Matthew 24:47). An earlier, and favorite, translation of many people reads this verse like this: "Verily I say unto you, that he shall make him ruler over all his goods" (Matthew 24:47, KJV). Now, why did Jesus have to assure those whom he has appointed to spiritual authority with this promise of making them ruler of all his goods if they feed his people the Word in its due season? Do you think he was offering them an incentive? Does the LORD of Glory have to bribe his faithful and wise servant? Maybe because this teaching is so vitally important, those who do as they are requested will be found worthy to receive rule over all his goods.

DON'T BE INDIFFERENT

Now Jesus makes a comment to those whom he has appointed to a position of spiritual authority and are *indifferent* to teaching the LORD's coming. Jesus says, "But if that evil servant should say in his heart, 'My LORD is delaying his coming,' and begins to beat his fellow-servants, and eat and drink with the drunken" (Matthew 24:48–49). Why did Jesus call his servant evil? He calls his servant evil because of what his servant says in his heart, which is, "My LORD is delaying his coming" (Matthew 24:48b). Speaking these words is in complete violation of the Word of God, because God has said the LORD's coming is near. "You also be patient. Establish your hearts, for the coming of the LORD is at hand" (James 5:8). If God says the catching away is at hand, then why would his servant contradict him? So what if it has been almost two thousand years since the Holy Spirit spoke this through James? As far as we are concerned, the LORD's coming is at hand. Many who have been put in a position of spiritual authority purposely neglect to teach little or anything about the catching away or the second coming. In their defense, it is likely because they themselves know little to nothing about these subjects; but I am not the one who has to stand in anyone's place but my own to give an account for that.

IT IS: WHAT'S IN THE HEART

The faithful and wise servant feeds the household of God their food in due season because they know the season of the LORD is coming. The *desire of his heart* is fully for the LORD's will, and he hears the Word of the LORD, therefore he is blessed. The evil servant does not recognize the season of the LORD's return because he has his own agenda, so he does not feed the household the right food in the right season. Therefore, the household does not have the right nourishment from the Word in order that they can be ready for the LORD's coming. Instead, this evil servant "beats his fellow-servants" (Matthew 24:49a), which means he does not physically beat them up, but he beats them up spiritually.

Beating the household of God up spiritually in this instance means the household is spiritually abused because of a lack of proper food (teaching in due season) about this great day. The evil servant takes advantage of his fellow servant and uses them for selfish gain, thinking "My LORD [LORD] is delaying his coming" (Matthew 24:48b). The evil servant "eats and drinks with the drunken" (Matthew 24:49b), which symbolically refers to a person who lives for this life instead of the kingdom of God. This servant might think he is doing the work of the kingdom, but how can one ignore the instructions from the owner of the kingdom and still be doing the owner's will? The evil servant does these things because he is convinced the LORD's return is a long way away, so he thinks he can just eat drink and be merry (live for this life). Just like in the days before the flood, people were eating and drinking, marrying and giving in marriage, up to the day Noah entered the ark.

THE CONSEQUENCES

The LORD has a harsh rebuke for someone he has given this great responsibility of spiritual authority to who has chosen not to use it to feed the household their food in due season. If this was not the season for the second coming of Christ and the catching away prior to that, then there would be no need to feed the household of God this particular diet. But when it is the season, and the LORD has said that he expects his servant to feed his household their food in due season, then who do we listen to? In verse fifty, Jesus says: "The LORD of that servant will come in a day when he doesn't expect it, and in an hour when he doesn't know it" (Matthew 24:50). Maybe you have heard some say that this means God will take them out before their time. They further explain this comment by saying, "God will somehow cause them to die," which I personally am not in agreement with. God does not cause his new creation to die before they have lived a long and abundant life, and whoever teaches this might try to prove it under the new covenant.

Let me try to prove what I am saying by beginning with a quote from the Book of Proverbs, which says: "Death and life are in the power of the tongue; those who love it will eat its fruit" (Proverbs 18:21). Death and life are in the power of *man's tongue,* so God is not going to take anyone out before their time. People take themselves out before their time, through *the power of their own tongue* and wrong choices. Wrong choices made by them and sometimes by someone else, which is by no means God's doing. This statement, I know, will fly in the face of many who have claimed that it was God's will when a loved one went prematurely; but I will recant my statement if you can prove your idea from the Word of God. And if you try to use the example of Ananias and his wife Sappphira from Acts chapter five, you might want to study the context of that story again. Ananias and Sapphire died because they lied to the Holy Spirit without repentance; therefore, they brought death to themselves by the power of their tongue. These two people died immediately, but how many have also brought death to themselves over a period of time because they did not appropriate God's grace and repent for lying to the Holy Spirit also?

What Jesus is saying in Matthew 24:50 is plain and simple to understand. Jesus will come in a day and an hour that this evil servant who belongs to him is not expecting or even ready for. This evil servant does not know the season or even consider with any sincere thought the day of the glorious appearing of the LORD. It is very important to remember that Jesus did say, "The LORD of that servant" (Matthew 24:50a). We see all through this passage that it is the LORD who puts this servant in charge of his household. Can someone whom the LORD has set over his household not obey him and then expect not to go astray?

The answer to this is found in 1 Samuel, where we read God instructed the Prophet Samuel to anoint Saul, son of Kish, of the tribe of Benjamin, as king over Israel.

God set King Saul over the House of Israel, the people of God, and because King Saul did not keep the commands of the LORD, God rejected Saul as king. So we do see that those whom the LORD has set over his household can have their own agenda, disobey the Word of God, and then go astray. The evil servant who says in his heart "My LORD is delaying his coming" (Matthew 24:48b), will definitely *not expect* the LORD to come on the day of his coming and he will *not even know the hour* it happens. This phrase "And in an hour when he doesn't know it" (Matthew 24:50b), likely means that when the catching away is taking place, this evil servant *will not have any idea* of what is going on. But that would mean he would not be part of the catching away, would it not? In the next chapter we will discuss this more closely.

Jesus: Always a Straight Talker

I don't know if you have noticed this about Jesus, but he never seems to hold anything back. When we read about his life and ministry, and with the record we have of the statements he's made, we see that he is very straightforward. He is a straight shooter. Jesus does not sugarcoat his words by being politically correct. He did not worry about hurting anyone's feelings by not saying things that might offend them. For example, what did Jesus call the Pharisees and some of the scribes when they found fault with the disciples when they saw them eating bread with unwashed hands? He called them hypocrites. "But he answering said to them, 'Well did Esaias [Isaiah] prophesy concerning you hypocrites, as it is written, 'This people honor me with their lips, but their heart is far away from me'" (Mark 7:6, Darby Translation). This is a cleverly straightforward remark to a people who expected everyone to bow before them.

Notice what Jesus says in verse fifty-one, concerning the evil servant: "And will cut him in pieces, and appoint his portion with the hypocrites; there is where the weeping and grinding of teeth will be" (Matthew 24:51). Jesus was not too worried about holding back his words to "the unfaithful." What began as criticism for the fault of not feeding the household of God their food in the right season, Jesus now brings a warning to the evil servant who says in his heart: "My Lord is delaying his coming" (Matthew 24:48b). This statement might offend the faint-hearted, but Jesus is more concerned with his servant's spiritual condition than he is in pricking their ego. Jesus is pronouncing a final judgment upon his servant whom he found not doing what they were supposed to be doing when he comes. Instead of this servant feeding the household of God their food in its due season—information of the catching away so their fellow servants can be watching to make themselves ready for it—they treat God's people with contempt. They beat their fellow servants, eat, and drink with the drunken, which is fellowshipping with the world, all because they think and say the LORD is delaying his coming.

JESUS APPOINTS

The LORD has just given signs of the time of his second coming, but the evil servant does not recognize the time or quite literally does not believe it. This is why the LORD calls this servant evil, because he does not believe the Word of the LORD. Therefore, the LORD says he will cut him in pieces, which has the implication of them being removed from their place within the household. This is similar to when the LORD says he will vomit out of his mouth those in the body of Christ who are *lukewarm* when he comes for his bride (see Revelation 3:10–11, 15–17).

Jesus says he will appoint the evil servant's portion with the hypocrites, which refers to them being appointed a place with other hypocrites. A hypocrite is someone who pretends to be someone they are not. When we study Luke chapter twelve, we see a portion of the parallel passage we are studying in Matthew chapter twenty-four. In Luke it says, "You hypocrites! You know how to interpret the appearance of the eretz [earth] and the sky, but how is it that you don't interpret this time?" (Luke 12:56). This refers to them not being able to interpret the signs of the time of the LORD's coming. Traditionally, this verse is always used to suggest the religious leaders of Jesus day did not recognize his first coming. But just as they did not recognize the LORD's first coming, there will be many kingdom officers who do not recognize his second coming either. The LORD says that the place of the hypocrites is where the weeping and grinding of teeth will be. What a horrible place this must be! We see this place of weeping and grinding of teeth also in Matthew 8:12, 22:13, and 25:30. Jesus says this is the place of outer darkness, which refers to the place outside of his glorious light.

MUCH TO CONSIDER

We can clearly see that all those whom the LORD appoints, or sets, over his household have very much to consider. Do they feed the household of God a diet that the LORD has not prescribed in these final days leading up to his coming? Do they ignore the signs of the time, which is an indicator that the household needs to be fed the proper food? Or does the servant of the LORD teach the household of God just whatever they desire, ignoring the menu the LORD has ordered? Are they faithful and wise servants who give the household their food in due season? If they are, then on the day the LORD catches away the church, they will be called blessed, and he will set them over all he owns. But if the faithful and wise servant decides that their agenda is greater than the LORD's, then they are evil and will be removed from their place within the household and be assigned a place with the hypocrites.

I have found multiple passages from Romans to the end of the Revelation that contain an enormous amount of verses that are a direct reference to the catching away of the church. I have inserted these passages in the last chapter and have entitled it *The Catching Away: References* so you can do further study. I have also included some commentary to help you with your study. We the church need to watch and be ready for the catching away because this day has been commissioned to complete our redemption. The second coming is the guideline for the catching away, so it is important that we know its timing so we can obey the LORD's command to watch and be ready for the catching away.

The Virgin's Lamp

We Have Personal Responsibility

Now that we have seen the great responsibility given to those whom the LORD has set over his household (kingdom officers) to teach the household to watch and be ready for the coming of the LORD, we now will discuss the responsibility the *household itself* has in this preparation. Yes, the body of Christ also has a responsibility to get *each one himself* ready for this glorious event. Even though it is the responsibility of the leaders to teach the body this Word in the right season, no Christian can lay blame on the leaders if they do not. We have seen in Matthew 24:45–51 that the LORD will deal with each one whom he has appointed to feed his sheep and who do not obey his instructions. So the house of God cannot accuse anyone, but we must take responsibility for what we are being fed. It is up to us individually to hear what the Spirit is saying.

We all have the Word of God before us to study and meditate on. If we have only the LORD's desire for our lives, then we will hear him more clearly than if we do not have desire for him. Many Christians are on a road that the LORD *is not* directing them on, thus they are candidates for going astray. Jesus says in the Gospel of John, "My sheep hear my voice, and I know them, and they follow me" (John 10:27). We need to put Jesus first in our life so the Holy Spirit can lead us, because it is written, "For as many as are led by the Spirit of God, these are children of God" (Romans 8:14).

We get insight into our responsibility as the body of Christ to be watching and ready for the catching away through the parable Jesus taught to his disciples about the ten virgins. Jesus and his disciples are still on the Mount of Olives, where he has been teaching them what signs there will be in the earth preceding his second coming with the reestablishment of the nation of Israel as the primary sign. Included also is critical information concerning the catching away of the church and what that day will be like.

Again, as a frame of reference, the method Jesus uses to teach his disciples about what it will be like when he comes for the church is with parabolic language. Initially, they would have no idea of what Jesus is really saying in this teaching. How could they? For at this point, they do not have the spiritual insight to understand what Jesus is referring to, especially because they had no idea of a church (made of Jews and Gentiles) and the catching away of it. It seems that Peter and John, along with the rest of the disciples, did not fully understand this parable until later on in their lives when they were in ministry building the household of God. By then, in addition to their knowledge comes the teaching of the apostle Paul (which the disciples would have received), in whom the LORD gave even *greater revelation* into the catching away of the body of Christ. Maybe Jesus did explain this parable to them, and we just have no record of it, but this is unlikely, considering the disciples were so confused when he was crucified.

JESUS TEACHES ABOUT THE VIRGINS

Let us first take a look at what Jesus taught the disciples about the two groups of people in the household of God, and then in chapter eleven of this book we will look into the day and the hour. Jesus says in Matthew chapter twenty-five:

> Then the Kingdom of Heaven will be like ten virgins, who took their lamps, and went out to meet the bridegroom. Five of them were foolish, and five were wise. Those who were foolish, when they took their lamps, took no oil with them, but the wise took oil in their vessels with their lamps.
>
> Matthew 25:1–4

Jesus begins in verse one by saying, "Then the Kingdom of Heaven will be like ten virgins, who took their lamps, and went out to meet the bridegroom" (Matthew 25:1). Jesus begins his parable with the word *then,* which functions as an adverb to denote a certain time. The *time* Jesus is referring to is the time of *his coming,* as he mentions no less than six times in his teaching about the catching away of the church in Matthew 24:37, 39, 42, 44, 46, and 50. So all Jesus is about to say in this parable relates to *the day* when he comes for the church. And the day Jesus comes for the church, "the Kingdom of Heaven ... will be like ... ten virgins who took their lamps, and went out to meet their bridegroom" (Matthew 25:1).

THE KINGDOM OF HEAVEN: THE KINGDOM OF GOD?

Why did Matthew write the term the *kingdom of heaven* instead of the *kingdom of God?* Is there any significance to it? The answer is no, because both terms are interchangeable. I mentioned this briefly in chapter one (*Why Parables?*). I know some people might argue and say each term has it own meaning. But let us look at one example of where these two terms are used interchangeably, and you can decide. The first example is in Matthew 13:11, where Matthew uses the term the "Kingdom of Heaven": "He [Jesus] answered them, "To you it is given to know the mysteries of the Kingdom of Heaven, but it is not given to them" (Matthew 13:11). The next example is in Luke 8:10, where Luke records the parallel passage as the "Kingdom of God": "To you it is given to know the mysteries of the Kingdom of God, but to the rest in parables; that 'seeing they may not see, and hearing they may not understand'" (Luke 8:10). Can you see where both authors are writing the same teaching of Jesus but using an interchangeable term to describe the same place? When we read through the Gospels, we see many other examples of this practice. In fact, when we do a study of this, we find Matthew uses the term "the Kingdom of Heaven" approximately thirty-one times, while both Mark and Luke use it zero times. Instead, Mark and Luke use the term "the Kingdom of God" fourteen and thirty-one times respectively, while Matthew uses it only three times. Both terms, "the Kingdom of God" and "the Kingdom of Heaven" mean the same thing, which is the *spiritual realm of God* and all aspects of it.

PHYSICAL VERSES SPIRITUAL

As we look further into this statement Jesus makes in Matthew 25:1 and still remember that he is using symbolic language, we see that this parable is *symbolic of a literal event*. The symbolism is that the virgins are about to meet their bridegroom, which represents *literally* the body of Christ who are about to meet the Christ. Symbolically, Jesus is referring to the body finally becoming one with him. Spiritually we are already one with

Jesus, as he is in us and we are in him because we belong to him, for it reads in 1 Corinthians, "But he who is joined to the LORD is one spirit" (1Corinthians 6:17). But physically we are apart from him, for it says in 2 Corinthians, "Being therefore always of good courage, and knowing that, while we are at home in the body, we are absent from the LORD" (2 Corinthians 5:6).

We cannot be one with Jesus physically until we receive our spiritual bodies, which will happen the day we are *taken up quickly* to meet the LORD in the air. Until then, we should be like the ten virgins *who are waiting* to meet their bridegroom, whom I would expect should be *longing* to be one with their husband. The body of Christ should have that excitement feeling (like a bride anticipating her wedding day) in the pit of our spirit of longing to be clothed with our spiritual body. For we read in 2 Corinthians chapter five: "For most assuredly in this we groan, longing to be clothed with our habitation, which is from heaven" (2 Corinthians 5:2). The habitation we will be clothed with is a *spiritually physical substance* that will allow us to become one with Jesus, who now dwells in the same spiritual physical substance.

This spiritual physical substance allows Jesus to be physically in the presence of God the Father, who is spirit, and allows Jesus to sit physically on his throne, at the Father's right hand in the heavenly realm. This throne was real enough for the apostle John to see it physically (while in the Spirit) as he states in Revelation: "Immediately I was in the Spirit. Behold, there was a throne set in heaven, and one sitting on the throne" (Revelation 4:2). We should remember that the LORD Jesus Christ is a man in a spiritually glorified body, as Paul says to Timothy: "For [there is] one God, and one mediator between God and men, the man Christ Jesus" (1 Timothy 2:5).

Just as a virgin becomes one with her bridegroom when they come together for the first time on their wedding day, the body of Christ will finally become *physically one* with Christ when we receive our heavenly habitation, which is our spiritual body, on the day the LORD catches us up. This spiritual body is referenced further in 1 Corinthians 15:35–54, where I encourage you to take a study of it.

MAKING THE TRANSITION

Jesus is teaching that there are ten virgins who took their lamps and went out to meet the bridegroom, which speaks of a wedding day. Symbolically, Jesus is referring to the body of Christ making the transition from the physical realm to the spiritual realm. This is the day when the trumpet of God will sound and those who have been asleep and those who are alive will rise to meet the LORD in the air. It is no coincidence that this parabolic teaching immediately follows his teaching from Matthew 24:36–51, which we learned is symbolic of the day and the hour of the catching away. This teaching is a symbolic picture of what it will be like on that very day and hour.

WE ARE THE BRIDE: REALLY!

The ten virgins represent the church, while the bridegroom represents the LORD Jesus himself. For those who doubt the relationship between Jesus and those who belong to him as being consistent with a bride and her bridegroom, let us look at what John the Baptist said. In the Gospel of John chapter three, we see where some of John the Baptist's disciples came to him complaining that all the people were beginning to go to Jesus to be baptized instead of to John. John says to his overly concerned disciples, "A man can receive nothing, unless it has been given him from heaven" (John 3:27). John also reminds them that he is not the Christ but only the one who was sent before the Christ. Then he makes this statement: "He who has the bride is the bridegroom; but the friend of the bridegroom, who stands and hears him, rejoices greatly because of the bridegroom's voice. This, my joy, therefore is made full" (John 3:29). What John said was that the people who come to Jesus are the bride, and he is the bridegroom. John is the friend of the bridegroom, and because he [John] hears the voice of the bridegroom, he [John] rejoices greatly.

Another example of the relationship between Jesus and his body as being consistent with a bride and her bridegroom can be found in 2 Corinthians, in which the Apostle Paul says, "For I am jealous over you with a godly jealousy. For I married you to one husband, in that I might present you as a pure virgin to Messiah [Christ]" (2 Corinthians 11:2). But some might say, *"I thought the New Jerusalem is the Lamb's bride."* When we do a study of Revelation chapter twenty-one, we see it does say this in verses nine and ten. But if you continue to read Revelation 21:12–14, you will notice this city has written on its twelve gates the names of the twelve tribes of Israel, along with twelve foundations, and on them are the twelve names of the twelve apostles of the Lamb. These twenty-four names represent the body of Christ, who will all be among those *caught up* to meet the LORD in the air on that glorious day.

This New Jerusalem is the place Jesus talked about to his disciples in the Gospel of John chapter fourteen when he said:

In my Father's house are many mansions. If it weren't so, I would have told you. I am going to prepare a place for you.

If I go and prepare a place for you, I will come again, and will receive you to myself; that where I am, you may be there also.

John 14:2–3

The New Jerusalem, which is called the "Holy City," is made by Jesus Christ for his bride. It seems like that this city will be the bride's wedding gift. Then in the future, at the right time, this Holy City will come down out of heaven to the earth for those who live on the earth as flesh and blood men and women to enjoy.

JESUS MAKES A POINT

Next Jesus says there are ten virgins, and the number ten is used by the LORD only to make a point; thus, it does not represent the total number of those consisting in the body of Christ. The virgin's lamps represent their *level of commitment* to the LORD and, by extension, their level of interest in being committed *to keep watch* (see Matthew 24:42; 25:13) and *to be ready* (see Matthew 24:44), because they do not know the day or the hour the LORD will come.

JESUS MAKES A COMPARISON

Jesus now gives a negative and positive description of this group of virgins, as he says, "Five of them were foolish, and five were wise" (Matthew 25:2). Jesus makes a comparison just as he did in Matthew chapter twenty-four, with the faithful and wise servants alongside those whom he called evil servants. One group of virgins is wise, and the other group of virgins is foolish. Symbolically, Jesus is making a comparison of those in the church who are wise and those in the church who are foolish. Is Jesus saying that the split between the wise and foolish are right down the middle, when he says five are foolish and five are wise? Once again, I believe he is only making a point of comparison with these figures.

The virgins that Jesus calls foolish do not have the same description as the group of Christians Paul called foolish in Galatians chapter three. "O foolish Galatians, who hath bewitched you that ye should not obey the truth, before whose eyes Jesus Christ hath been evidently set forth, crucified among you?" (Galatians 3:1, KJV). The Greek word Paul uses to describe those in the Galatia church who were foolish has the meaning of not being able to comprehend or simply not using their head to think. But the word Matthew uses to describe what Jesus meant when he called these virgins foolish has a different meaning altogether. It has what seems to be a condemning tone to it. The word Jesus used when he called these virgins foolish has the meaning of *being godless* or having *no reverence* for God (when it is used to refer to a person; when used to refer to things, it has the meaning of being stupid. Here Jesus is referring to the person and not to things). Was Jesus saying that these foolish or godless virgins have *no reverential fear* for their bridegroom? Yes, he was! But also keep in mind that this parable symbolizes him and his church. So what Jesus is saying is that the five foolish virgins, who symbolically represent a portion of the church, do not acknowledge him because they are godless. They do not fear the LORD, which is the beginning of wisdom. Matthew records this same Greek word for *foolish* when Jesus taught the crowds in the Sermon on the Mount. Jesus said, "Everyone who hears these words of mine and doesn't do them will be like a foolish (ungodly) man who built his house on the sand" (Matthew 7:26).

THE OIL

Jesus goes on to say, "Those who were foolish, when they took their lamps, took no oil with them, but the wise took oil in their vessels with their lamps" (Matthew 25:3–4). Remember, the virgin's *lamps symbolically represent their commitment* to the LORD, which extends to their level of interest in *watching and being ready* for his coming for them. The oil represents *the substance that empowers the virgin's commitment* to the bridegroom, which is their faith. Some may oppose this symbol and say that the oil represents the Holy Spirit. Yes, oil does symbolically represent the Holy Spirit in Scripture, but that is specific anointing oil. The oil that Jesus mentions here is straight olive oil used for burning in lamps. Anointing oil is different in that its base is olive oil with four specific spices mixed with the olive oil to make sacred anointing oil. You can find the ingredients to anointing oil in Exodus 30:22–25.

So where can we find some evidence that this oil Jesus is referring to symbolically refers to the virgin's faith? In Genesis 28:10–22 we see the story of Jacob dreaming of a stairway set up on the earth, with the top of it reaching to heaven and the angels of God are ascending and descending on it. Jacob envisions the LORD at the top of the stairway, in which the LORD begins to make Jacob some promises. The LORD tells Jacob, as he lay there with his head on a stone, that he will give Jacob and his seed the land where he is lying. Jacob's seed will be as the dust of the earth, and he will spread abroad to the west and to the east and to the north and to the south. In Jacob and his seed, the LORD will bless all the families of the earth. The LORD will keep Jacob wherever he goes and will bring Jacob back into this land. We see that when Jacob awoke, he knew he had met with the LORD.

Genesis chapter twenty-eight says that Jacob "rose up early in the morning, and took the stone that he had put under his head, and set it up for a pillar, and poured oil on the top of it" (Genesis 28:18). Pouring the oil on the stone that Jacob set up for a pillar was a *physical gesture of Jacob's faith* in what God had just promised him. This action symbolically represents Jacobs's belief that what God just spoke to him, he believes. So pouring the oil, which was straight olive oil used for burning in lamps, was an *outward physical action* of what Jacob believed in the depth of his spirit.

Another example of this is in Genesis chapter thirty-five: "Ya`akov [Jacob] set up a pillar in the place where he [God] spoke with him, a pillar of stone. He poured out a drink-offering on it, and poured oil on it" (Genesis 35:14). Again, Jacob pours oil (and a drink offering) on the stone pillar that he set up where God talked to him. In verse ten we see God changed Jacob's name to Israel, and then he proceeded to tell Jacob that nations and kings will come from his loins. In verse thirteen, God tells Jacob that the land he gave to Abraham and Isaac he gives to Jacob and his descendants. The pouring of the *straight olive oil* on the stone pillar Jacob set up, at the place where God said these things to him, was another *act of faith*. It represented a physical manifestation of Jacob's faith in the promises God just made to him.

Some will say that Jacob's actions in pouring the oil on the stone in both these incidents were only to consecrate the place where God spoke to him. Yes, anyone who suggests this is right because Jacob was consecrating theses places where God spoke to him and made these promises both times. But for Jacob to pour the oil out, to consecrate the place where God spoke to him, took a measure of faith. If Jacob had not believed what God spoke to him, he would not have poured the oil out over the stones to consecrate these special places. But because Jacob *did* believe what God spoke to him, he poured the oil out, which was a physical manifestation of his faith in the Word of God. Jacob devoted both these places where God gave him his word, which took an act of faith in believing the word spoken to him in which the oil was a physical manifestation of Jacob's faith.

In these two passages, the oil symbolically represents Jacobs's faith to believe the Word of God that was spoken to him. Because Jacob believes the Word of God, he consecrates or devotes these portions of land to the LORD. Jacob's actions were produced by a spirit of faith. It reads in 2 Corinthians chapter four, "But having the same spirit of faith, according to that which is written, 'I believed, and therefore I spoke.' We also believe, and therefore also we speak" (2 Corinthians 4:13). This is how the Christian manifests faith; we speak what we believe (which should be the Word of God only). If we believe the Word of God, we will speak it. Jacob's pouring out of the oil was a physical gesture of faith. He believed what God promised, so as a manifestation of faith Jacob pours out the oil to consecrate these places. The oil symbolically did the speaking for Jacob.

The foolish virgin's level of commitment to the LORD in keeping watch and being ready was not empowered by faith in God's teaching to them. They took their lamps but did not take any oil with them. Their commitment to the LORD's coming was not accompanied by faith.

The Faithful: Pick up the Slack

We said in the previous chapter that it is the responsibility of those whom the Lord has set over his household, namely the teacher and the preacher, to teach the Lord's coming in its due season. They are to teach this subject to get God's people ready for the Lord's return, because a bride always has to be ready for when the bridegroom comes for her. Now we know that not all the faithful and wise servants who have been called will feed the household of God their food in its due season, or Jesus would not have described some of them as being evil. Just to refresh our memories, Jesus gives us the reason why he calls them evil: "But if that evil servant should say in his heart, 'My Lord is delaying his coming'" (Matthew 24:48). Just because there will be those who will be negligent in teaching and preaching the coming of the Lord and getting the church ready, does not mean the Lord himself will neglect the body. He will make sure his household gets their food (the right food) in due season through those servants who are faithful and wise. The faithful and wise may have to work a bit harder to pick up the slack, but remember what the Lord's promise to them is: "Blessed is that servant whom his Lord finds doing so when he comes. Most assuredly I tell you that he will set him over all that he has" (Matthew 24:46–47).

No Mixture

The problem with the foolish virgin in Jesus's teaching *is not* that they are not getting their food in its due season; their problem is they are not mixing their food (the Word of God) with faith. They are short on oil! The foolish Christian does not mix the Word of God with faith as it says in the Book of Hebrews: "For indeed we have had good news preached to us, even as they also did, but the Word they heard didn't profit them, because it wasn't mixed with faith by those who heard" (Hebrews 4:2). We typically hear this verse quoted and referred to only those who are not born again through the power of the Holy Spirit. But this verse also has relevance for those who have been delivered from the world. The "good news" is *all things* that pertain to our salvation and not just the initial information one needs to get saved. For example, the "good news" also refers to the solid information that Jesus is coming for those who are waiting for him (see chapter sixteen: *The Catching Away: References*).

We see in Hebrews chapter three that the writer is saying that it is Israel, the people of God, who did not mix the Word of God with faith. We see from Hebrews that these people (a whole generation of them) who were delivered from Egypt (a type of the world) were not able to enter the rest of God because they hardened their hearts. The Hebrew elders were constantly testing the patience of the LORD for forty years, and the LORD says, "Therefore, I was displeased with that generation, and said, 'They always err in their heart, but they didn't know my ways;' as I swore in my wrath, 'They will not enter into my rest'" (Hebrews 3:10–11). I can imagine some people saying now, "See! That was Israel." But we see the writer of Hebrews says to the Christian, "Beware, brothers, lest perhaps there be in any one of you an evil heart of unbelief, in falling away from the living God" (Hebrews 3:12). So we see that even the Christian can have a heart that is unbelieving.

SOME PICK AND CHOOSE

Many Christians have a problem with believing what God says in his Word on a number of subjects, especially watching and being ready for his coming. Many Christians pick and choose what subjects in the Bible they choose to believe and live by. The other subjects they choose to not think about and sometimes will actually persecute those who do teach them. The foolish virgins in Jesus's parable had lamps, which symbolically represent commitment, but they took no oil with them, which symbolically represents lack of faith. They would have been taught to watch and be ready for the day of the LORD, but they did not believe it enough to be committed to it. In fact, they make up their own theologies, which consist of well-known phrases like, "I know about the LORD's coming, but it will come whenever it comes." Their idea is to just live day to day because the catching away of the church will never happen in their lifetime (so they hope). This actually is an earthly theology that foolish (ungodly) virgins live by.

FAITH EMPOWERS COMMITMENT

We can see in Jesus's parable the wise virgin's level of commitment was huge because it was empowered by faith. They took oil in their vessels along with their lamps, which means they continued to feed and meditate on the Word of God and believe it. A wise virgin knows they have to be watching and be ready because they do not know the day or the hour their LORD will come. The wise virgins in this story took extra oil along with them because they did not want their lamps (commitment) to go out, as we will see in the upcoming chapter. The wise virgins knew enough that if they were insufficient in their levels of oil, their lamps would burn out. Symbolically, it has reference to our faith being at the right level so our commitment to the LORD will not dry up.

So many have let their commitment to the LORD dry up due to the fact their level of faith is insufficient. It says in Romans chapter ten, "So faith comes by hearing, and hearing by the Word of God"

(Romans 10:17). The only way our level of faith will be sufficient is to continually hear and study the Word of God. Therefore, it is imperative the Christian continually feed on the Word of God so that their spirit be thoroughly nourished with faith.

No Oil

So far we have learned that it is foolish for the virgin not to have enough oil to replenish their lamp, where a wise virgin will make sure they take oil in their vessel for their lamp. Symbolically speaking, a foolish Christian will be lacking in faith to the promises of the LORD's coming for his church, where a wise Christian will be looking for the LORD's return with absolute expectancy.

Faith in His Coming

What does it mean to be lacking in faith concerning the promises of the LORD's return for his church? First, it means the foolish Christian lacks the substance [faith] it takes to even hope for the promises of God pertaining to the catching away of the body of Christ. The writer of Hebrews, by the inspiration of the Holy Spirit, says, "Now faith is the substance of things hoped for, the evidence of things not seen" (Hebrews 11:1, KJV). We also see that everyone who has put their hope in the LORD's appearing purifies themselves, as it says in 1 John:

> Beloved, now we are children of God, and it is not yet revealed what we will be. But we know that, when he is revealed, we will be like him; for we will see him just as he

is. Everyone who has this hope set on him purifies himself, even as he is pure.

1 John 3:2–3

A Christian can have *no hope* (in their heart) for the LORD's appearing if they do not have *the faith* in which to believe it. Many will say, "But I do believe in the LORD's coming!" I say that your faith is dead unless your actions prove otherwise. What I mean by this is, if we are not preparing ourselves now, in this due season, then we really do not believe it is the due season for the catching away. There is no manifestation of faith because there is no hope. Do we have to prepare ourselves for the coming of the LORD? Does it really matter? If it does not matter, then Jesus was in error to give these three separate commands:

Watch therefore.

Matthew 24:42a

Therefore also be ready.

Matthew 24:44a

Watch therefore, for you don't know the day nor the hour in which the Son of Man is coming.

Matthew 25:13

Secondly, to be lacking in faith concerning the promises of the LORD's return means that the foolish Christian believes they have no evidence that the catching away will happen in their lifetime. They have no evidence, because they have no faith.

Faith is the evidence of things not seen. They believe they have no evidence because they fail to see it in God's Word.

Many Christians will rise up on their podium made of sand and say, "How are we supposed to believe this is the due season, when there are so many different theories being taught?" I will rebut with what we have discussed earlier in this book. We have learned that Jesus spoke in parables for a specific reason, because the parables contain *the mysteries* of the kingdom. Again, it bears repeating: "To you it is given to know the mysteries of the Kingdom of Heaven, but it is not given to them" (Matthew 13:11). I will venture to say that everyone's lack of the substance or the faith to even hope for the catching away in this due season is because the catching away and its timing is one of the mysteries of the kingdom of God. This is why Jesus spoke of the timing of his second coming in parabolic language in Matthew 24:32–35. The coming of the LORD for his church is not a message for just anyone. It has been given to those who have ears to hear and eyes to see.

If we belong to the LORD, then we have ears and eyes that have the *potential* to hear and see what the Spirit is saying. But just like Peter, James, Andrew, John, and the rest of the first disciples, we need to be taught correctly. Remember, if anyone is born again, the Holy Spirit will bear witness with our spirit that what is being taught is either from God or just from man's own ideas. So if anyone who is reading this book lacks the faith concerning the promises of the LORD's coming, in this due season, then dig in and study what the Holy Spirit has given. He will tell you if you truly desire his truth.

It Seems Like Forever!

We should continue now and discuss what happened to the five foolish virgins and the five wise virgins in Jesus's teaching.

> Now while the bridegroom delayed, they all slumbered and slept. But at midnight there was a cry, 'Behold! The bridegroom is coming! Come out to meet him!' Then all those virgins arose, and trimmed their lamps. The foolish said to the wise, 'Give us some of your oil, for our lamps are going out.' But the wise answered, saying, 'What if there isn't enough for us and you? You go rather to those who sell, and buy for yourselves.'
>
> Matthew 25:5–13

We see in verse five it says: "Now while the bridegroom delayed, they all slumbered and slept" (Matthew 25:5). All the virgins knew the bridegroom was coming for them, but to them he was taking such a long time, so they all began to get tired and fell asleep. This is symbolic of the last days prior to the catching away, when it seems that forever we have heard of the soon return of Christ, but because it has not happened yet Christians begin to think it will never happen.

Some Begin to Yawn

Verse five on the exterior can be somewhat misleading. As we give it a quick glance, when it says "the virgins slumbered" or "began to get tired," we get the impression with the language being used that their heads became too heavy and began to drop because they were getting sleepy. Then they fell asleep. But remember, Jesus is teaching a symbolic message that can only be understood with those who have understanding. On the surface, Jesus is using parabolic language to teach about ten virgins who were waiting for their bridegroom to come. Beneath the surface of this message Jesus is teaching about his bride waiting for him to come. When Jesus says all the virgins began to slumber and fall asleep, he was not referring to them nodding off and falling into natural sleep. Jesus is saying, as it refers to the church, that because of his delay they will begin to get *apathetic, even negligent* toward his coming. And because they begin to get apathetic toward his coming, they begin to sleep, meaning they have become *indifferent* to spiritual things, especially the message of the catching away.

As an example, the apostle Paul says to the Thessalonians, "So then let's not sleep, as the rest do, but let's watch and be sober" (1 Thessalonians 5:6). Paul was telling the Thessalonians, along with all the church, in this passage *not to be indifferent* about the LORD's coming like those who do not care. He says the day of the LORD will come like a thief in the night but only to those who are in darkness. Those who are not in darkness, the day of the LORD will not overtake them like a thief, because they are sons of the light, and they will not be caught off guard because of their preparation. So Paul encourages the sons of the light not to sleep, or be indifferent, as those in darkness concerning the coming of the LORD. (See 1 Thessalonians 5:1–11.)

SOME GET CRITICAL

Some of the slumbering virgins were likely even making comments of mockery, like in 2 Peter where it says, "Where is the promise of his coming?" (2 Peter 3:4a). If you take a look at 2 Peter, in chapter three you will see that these people who were questioning the LORD's coming are Christians. Peter says there shall come in the last days, prior to the coming of the LORD for his church, scoffers who will walk after their own lusts instead of preparing themselves for the LORD. Their faith in the LORD's coming is obviously low or even nonexistent because the bridegroom is delaying. They get tired of waiting for him and start to engage in other things. As we will see, the foolish virgins were more concerned with their own agenda instead of their bridegrooms coming.

IT'S TIME!

Jesus goes on to say, "But at midnight there was a cry, 'Behold! The bridegroom is coming! Come out to meet him!' Then all those virgins arose, and trimmed their lamps" (Matthew 25:6–7). The cry is made at midnight, sounding the alarm that the bridegroom is coming, which literally means, "He is here! Come out to meet him!" The word Matthew uses for cry in this verse refers to a loud cry or noisy shouting, indicating there was intense emotion behind it. The likely reason for this intense emotion is because there is no more time to prepare, because the bridegroom is here. It can be compared with the days of Noah, when the floods came; there was no more time to prepare. There was not another year or month or day or hour of preparation time left. The flood came and took them all away.

All the virgins arose from their sleep, which symbolically refers to them arising from their apathy. Their lack of interest in the bridegroom's coming has now come to an abrupt end. This is now the hour, as midnight would suggest. The day and the hour of the LORD's coming for his church is being symbolically referred to here, although I am not predicting the hour of the catching away to be at twelve midnight.

Any Commitment: Any Faith?

Jesus continues: "Then all those virgins arose, and trimmed their lamps" (Matthew 25:7). Remember their lamps symbolically refer to their commitment. The trimming of their lamps refers to the strength of their commitment. Had all the virgins built their commitment to the LORD through faith? Was there enough oil in each virgin's lamp so it would not go out? The virgins knew the bridegroom was coming, but did they all have enough oil in their lamps? This symbolically means, "Did they have enough faith to believe it and be ready before it was too late?"

It looks like the foolish virgins did not have enough oil, as we read in verse eight: "The foolish said to the wise, 'Give us some of your oil, for our lamps are going out'" (Matthew 25:8). The foolish virgins realize only now they don't have enough oil. They realize only now that their faith is not where it should be in the LORD. The foolish virgins say, "Our lamps are going out" (Matthew 25:8b), because they did not take any oil with them. They don't have sufficient faith to keep their commitment burning or to keep it strong. The foolish virgins commitment to their bridegroom has been proven unworthy, because their lamps are going out due to a lack of oil, which represents their faith. They spent their time in unbelief instead of watching and being ready for the bridegroom. The foolish virgins are not ready to meet their bridegroom. The foolish virgins even ask the wise virgins for some of their oil, meaning some of their faith, thinking they will get an instant commitment boost. Because the foolish virgins did not properly prepare themselves for the bridegroom, it indicates they were unfaithful to him.

They Don't Care

What virgin lays in wait for her bridegroom and then when he comes, is not ready for him? A virgin who is unworthy of her bridegroom, that's who. These particular virgins, in Jesus teaching, did not have enough commitment to sustain them, because their bridegroom *was taking too long* to come for them, or so it seemed to them. Their commitment was not strong enough to sustain them due to a shortfall of faith. When we look beneath the surface of this parable, the main point of Christ's teaching involves faith and commitment because he exhorts his readers to, "Watch therefore, for you don't know the day or the hour in which the Son of Man is coming" (Matthew 25:13). It was the foolish virgin's responsibility to replenish the oil in their lamps. How did they think their lamp would burn to give them light with no oil?

We Need to Replenish

When we compare this to the life of the Christian, the only way we can replenish our oil to keep our lamp burning, so we can have light instead of darkness, is to continually replenish the Word of God into our spirit. I repeat what Paul wrote in Romans: "So faith comes by hearing, and hearing by the Word of God" (Romans 10:17). Nourishing our spirit with the Word of God is the only way faith comes and increases. Faith does not come through trials and tribulation as so many think. These things test the faith we might already have, but faith does not come because of them. As compared to the virgins in Jesus teaching, the only way the Christian can stay committed to the Lord is through faith replenished. Our faith in God and what he says has to be continually replenished so our commitment to him never diminishes but only increases.

WE CANNOT REPLENISH SOMEONE ELSE'S VESSEL

The wise virgins reply to the foolish virgin's request: "But the wise answered, saying, 'What if there isn't enough for us and you? You go rather to those who sell, and buy for yourselves'" (Matthew 25:9). The wise virgins knew they had enough oil for themselves but were unsure if what they had would be enough for the foolish. It sounds like they would help if they could. The wise virgins knew the bridegroom was delaying his coming, which is why they made sure they had enough oil. Both groups did not know the day and the hour of the bridegroom's return, but only the wise made sure they had sufficient amounts of oil to keep their lamps burning.

The Christian cannot live off his brother or sister's faith. He and she must make sure they have sufficient amounts of faith to fuel their commitment to the LORD. We must plant the Word of God daily into our spirit to keep it nourished. If the Christian is not kept nourished with the Word of God, our commitment to the LORD and his will, will surely get weak and die. Yes, there is the danger of the Christian not continuing in the faith to which we were called. The apostle Paul said this in Colossians chapter one:

> And you, that were formerly alienated and enemies in [your] mind by wicked works, yet now hath he reconciled, In the body of his flesh through death, to present you holy and unblamable and unreprovable in his sight: If ye continue in the faith grounded and settled, and [are] not moved away from the hope of the gospel, which ye have heard, [and] which hath been preached to every creature which is under heaven; of which I Paul am made a minister.
>
> Colossians 1:21–23 (Webster's Bible)

Paul warns the church that even though we have been reconciled or restored to right standing with God, we must continue in the faith, staying grounded and settled in it.

This is also what it says in Acts:

> When they had preached the Good News to that city, and had made many talmidim [disciples], they returned to Lystra, Iconium, and Antioch, confirming the souls of the talmidim [disciples], exhorting them to continue in the faith, and that through many afflictions we must enter into the Kingdom of God.
>
> Acts 14:21–22

When Paul and Barnabas went to the city of Derbe, they preached the gospel message and won many to the LORD. It says in this passage that they also had to exhort the new disciples to "continue in the faith" (Acts 14:22b).

WE MUST CONTINUE

Now if someone is born again by the Spirit of God, why must they be strongly urged to continue in the faith? Are we not saved by grace through faith? Yes, we are saved by God's grace through faith in the LORD, Jesus Christ, but *we must continue* in it. We must stay "grounded and settled" (Colossians 1:23b, Webster's Bible) in it. The writer of Hebrews says this in Hebrews chapter three:

> Messiah [Christ] is faithful as a Son over his house; whose house we are, if we hold fast our confidence and the glorying of our hope firm to the end. For we have become par-

takers of Messiah [Christ], if we hold fast the beginning of our confidence firm to the end.

Hebrews 3:6, 14

Please pay close attention to what it just said here! It said we are God's house: "if we hold fast our confidence and the glory of our hope firm to the end" (Hebrews 3:6c). It also says we are partakers of Christ "if we hold fast the beginning of our confidence firm to the end" (Hebrews 3:14b). In other words, *we must hold fast to our faith* in Christ and his Words firm *to the end of our physical life,* or the church age, whichever comes first. We are to be strong in the LORD as Paul said. "Watch! Stand firm in the faith! Be courageous! Be strong!" (1 Corinthians 16:13). Which I also add, be committed to him!

It Is a Process, You Know

The foolish virgins in this teaching by the LORD Jesus are a type of those who do not hold fast their confidence, which they had at the beginning. They do not continue in the faith firmly until the end of their salvation process. Salvation is a process, you know. The Christian is not fully redeemed until the day when the body of Christ is caught away, as it says in Romans: "Not only so, but ourselves also, who have the first fruits of the Spirit, even we ourselves groan within ourselves, waiting for adoption, the redemption of our body" (Romans 8:23). Our spirit was made new the moment we were born again, just as if our spirit had never sinned, but then we go through a transformation process. From the time we were made new creations, until the time of the catching away, we are to present our bodies as a living sacrifice, holy and acceptable to God, and renew our mind to the Word of God to continue the transformation process. Paul urged the Christians in Rome with this Word:

> Therefore I urge you, brothers, by the mercies of God, to present your bodies a living sacrifice, holy, acceptable to God, which is your spiritual service. Don't be conformed to this world, but be transformed by the renewing of your mind, so that you may prove what is the good and acceptable and perfect will of God."
>
> Romans 12:1–2

So from the time a Christian becomes born again by the power of grace through faith until the time we are fully redeemed, we must hold fast to the confidence we had at the beginning of our salvation and "continue in the faith" until the end of our life on this earth.

THROUGH TO THE END

We can see the underlying message in this teaching parable is that it takes commitment to the LORD to *stay with him* until the day he comes for the church. The wise virgins say the only thing they can say to the foolish group, which is, "You go rather to those who sell, and buy for yourselves" (Matthew 25:9b). This is symbolically referring to getting faith through the Word of God. The Christian can only get faith from hearing and hearing the Word of God. No Christian can get faith from someone else's faith. A Christian's faith will not rub off on anyone. Oh yes. Inspiration can rub off on someone else. A person can be inspired by someone else's faith, but we cannot get some of their faith. A person cannot use someone else's oil (faith) to keep their lamp (commitment) from burning out. If a Christian does not have enough oil for their own lamp, their commitment to the LORD will go out. Initially, the Christian has to have some faith, or he and she would not have been redeemed. But as these foolish virgins symbolically reveal, even this measure of faith can begin to diminish if it is not replenished.

The Door Was Shut

The Christian must continue *in the faith* to which he and she was called. We cannot be half dedicated to the LORD and half dedicated to ourselves. Our dedication to him cannot be in between. The LORD calls this being lukewarm. The LORD Jesus Christ makes a straightforward statement in the message he gave to the apostle John for him then to write to one of the seven churches in the *Revelation of Jesus Christ*. Jesus gave this warning with the intention of there being a turn around in the hearts of his people. Jesus says this in Revelation chapter three:

> I know your works, that you are neither cold nor hot. I wish you were cold or hot. So, because you are lukewarm, and neither hot nor cold, I will vomit you out of my mouth. Because you say, "I am rich, and have gotten riches, and have need of nothing;" and don't know that you are the wretched one, miserable, poor, blind, and naked.
>
> Revelation 3:15–17

Jesus found this group neither cold nor hot in their commitment to him. All through the age of the church he has found some Christians this way. This group can be found more alive today than at any other time with some of the statements Paul prophecies in his writings, which we will look at as we go further along. This group of lukewarm believers may be among those whom Jesus referred to as foolish virgins.

WHEN THE BRIDEGROOM ARRIVES

We continue with Jesus's parable in verse ten: "While they went away to buy, the bridegroom came, and those who were ready went in with him to the marriage feast, and the door was shut" (Matthew 25:10). When the bridegroom is about to arrive, it is not the time to be out buying oil. At the time of the catching away of the church, the Christian better have faith as we read in Luke, "Nevertheless, when the Son of Man comes, will he find faith on the eretz [earth]?" (Luke18:8b). While the foolish virgins were out frantically replenishing their oil levels, the bridegroom came. We do not know if these foolish virgins ever did replenish their oil levels, only that they went away to buy after they were told to. We only see them coming, in verse eleven, looking to get in after the door was shut. The wise virgins went in with the bridegroom to the marriage feast because they were *ready and waiting* for him. After the wise virgins were inside where the wedding banquet was taking place, the door was shut.

One moment after the LORD comes and the body of Christ is caught up to meet the LORD in the air, the door to the church of the LORD Jesus Christ will be shut. There will be no more added to the number of the church, because the church age will be finished. Oh yes, there will be people in the tribulation period who will repent of their sins and turn to God—multiple hundreds of millions, in fact—but they will not be among those who make up the body of Christ. Those who are saved in the Tribulation period are called the saints of God also, but we see their position in Christ will be different than those who make up the body of Christ. The LORD Jesus Christ sits at the right hand of his Father in heaven, as it says in Ephesians:

> (God) raised him (Jesus) from the dead, and made him to sit at his right hand in the heavenly places, far above all rule, and authority, and power, and dominion, and every name that is named, not only in this world, but also in that which is to come.
>
> Ephesians 1:20b-21

The body of Christ has been given the place to sit with Christ on his throne in the kingdom of God. Ephesians also says this: "(God) raised us up with him (Jesus), and made us to sit with him in the heavenly places in Messiah [Christ] Yeshua, [Jesus]" (Ephesians 2:6).

WHERE IS THE KINGDOM OF GOD?
The kingdom of God originates in the spiritual dimension unseen with the physical eye and extends into this physical world in the spirits of those who are born again. One day the kingdom of God will extend to fill the earth completely. In a spiritual sense, we the body of Christ are seated with Christ at the right hand of God now, but after we receive our spiritual bodies we will be there physically. Does this mean the multiple hundreds of millions of us who are in the body of Christ sit on his specific throne literally? What this means is that the Messiah's throne, which is his and his alone, is the place were he rules all authorities, powers, and dominion whether physical or spiritual. Our Father, because of his grace toward us, has allowed us to share in what he has given to Christ because we are heirs of God and joint-heirs with the Christ *if we suffer with our* LORD, that we

may be glorified together (see Romans 8:17). We share in all that has been given to Christ Jesus, although he is the Head over every power and authority.

We who are Christ's body rule with him over every power and authority in this age and in the age to come. This means the body of Christ has his authority and power over those in the spiritual places right now and in eternity. We rule with Christ now in the spiritual places, which extends into this earth, and in the spiritual places after we are given our spiritual body. We do not see this position given to those who are saved in the Tribulation period, even though many will be killed because of Christ; but we do see them ruling with Christ *on the earth only*, after the seventieth week of Israel is complete.

GLORIFIED SPIRITUAL BODIES

We see in Revelation 6:9–11 the souls of those who are martyred in the Tribulation are being given white robes, which represents righteousness, but there is no mention of them being seated with Christ in the heavenly places. The body of Christ receives *glorified spiritual bodies* like that of the LORD Jesus Christ when the LORD comes, as we see in 1 Corinthians 15:50–54, 2 Corinthians 5:1–5, and 1 John 3:2–3. We do not read any place where the Tribulation saints are given glorified spiritual bodies, although we see the Tribulation saints being raised up to life at *the first resurrection* where they will reign with Christ for 1,000 years (the millennial reign of Christ). They will be priests of God and of Christ, as we also see in Revelation 20:4–6.

But it does not say that this group receive glorified spiritual bodies, as it does *specifically* of those who are caught up to meet the LORD in the air before the Tribulation period. So we must assume these resurrected saints will be resurrected into flesh-

and-blood bodies just like Lazarus, the dear friend of Jesus, in John 11:38–44. The Tribulation saints will be priests of God and of Christ and will reign with him on the earth for 1,000 years in flesh-and-blood bodies just like they have now. They will live in these flesh-and-blood bodies forever, just like man was supposed to when God made Adam.

Like I stated before, only the body of Christ will receive glorified spiritual bodies at the moment of the catching away, which will complete our salvation making us fully redeemed. Even those who have already passed on in Christ, known as the dead in Christ, will have their earthly bodies resurrected at this time so they can receive their spiritual body. At this point, the faithful ones who have fallen asleep *are not* fully redeemed. Those in the body of Christ who have passed on before us like Paul, Peter, John, and all the faithful ones are not yet fully redeemed. Being fully redeemed means that all the body of Christ receives their glorified spiritual body at the same time so we can be like Jesus, just as he is (See 1 John 3:2–3).

THERE IS A DISTINCTION

The Man Jesus Christ, who is mediator between God (the Father) and men, is in his glorified spiritual body already. It is written in 1 Corinthians 15:49: "And as we have borne the image of the [one] made of dust, we shall bear also the image of the heavenly [one]" (Darby Translation). The dead in Christ are resurrected at the time of the *pre-Tribulation* catching away, instead of the first resurrection (see Revelation 20:4–6), because they were destined for glorified spiritual bodies instead of earthly bodies that shall never die. Only the body of Christ, who has been made a new creation, is given a body like the LORD Jesus Christ, which is a glorified spiritual body. If this is not so, then why in God's plan are those who are dead in Christ resurrected at the catching away along with those still living? Why would God the Father not just resurrect them at the first resurrection with the Tribulation saints? Why does the Bible call the resurrection of the Tribulation saints "the first resurrection" when already there has been a resurrection of the dead in Christ at the coming of the LORD for the body of Christ? The answer to these questions is that there is *a distinction* between the body of Christ and the Tribulation saints. Both groups are sanctified (made holy and separated from the world) unto God, but both are different. The distinction is that the body of Christ is given glorified spiritual bodies so we can sit with Christ in the heavenly places in the age to come, as we do now, and continue to reign with him over the spiritual things in the spiritual places. We will, of course, have spiritual authority with Jesus on the earth after the Great Tribulation. The Tribulation saints will be resurrected into earthly bodies so they can reign with Christ on the earth for one thousand years. The body of Christ will have access both in the spiritual places and the earth because we are clothed with glorified spiritual bodies. The Tribulation saints will have access to the earth only, because they are clothed with resurrected physical bodies.

CONTINUED COMMITMENT

The LORD continues with his teaching about the virgins: "Afterward the other virgins also came, saying, 'LORD, LORD, open to us.' But he answered, 'Most assuredly I tell you, I don't know you'" (Matthew 25:11–12). After the door was shut to the marriage feast, the foolish virgins came and wanted in. But the bridegroom says *he does not know them.* Now why would the bridegroom say this to the virgins who were betrothed to him?

Did they not at least make the effort to go at the very last minute to get fully prepared for his coming? And then in return for their effort, he says he does not know them! Remember that this teaching parable symbolically represents the church as the bride of Christ. Symbolically this teaching reveals to us that there are *two groups* in the church. There is the wise group who prepares themselves for the LORD by *continuing in the faith* to which they have been called and *staying committed* to him. Then there is the foolish group who *does not* continue in the faith; therefore, their commitment to the LORD goes out like a lamp that runs out of oil.

The body of Christ includes all those who continued in the faith and were committed to Christ until the day they died physically. It also includes those who are still alive and continue in the faith being committed to Christ even up until the day and the hour of the catching away. Then those who have fallen asleep in Christ and we who are alive in Christ will meet the LORD in the atmosphere together and be with him forever. The dead in Christ also includes the Old Testament saints who put their faith in the Anointed One and were committed to him even before he came in the flesh.

COMMITTED WITHOUT KNOWING HIM

The Old Testament saints put their faith in the Word of God concerning their Messiah's coming and were committed to him without even seeing him or knowing who he was. Hebrews chapter eleven speaks about some of the saints who lived before Christ came the first time. It says this about them:

> All these died in faith, not having received the promises,
> but having seen them from afar off and embraced [them],

and confessed that they were strangers and sojourners on the earth. But now they seek a better, that is, a heavenly; wherefore God is not ashamed of them, to be called their God; for he has prepared for them a city. And these all, having obtained witness through faith, did not receive the promise, God having foreseen some better thing for us, that they should not be made perfect without us.

Hebrews 11:13, 16, 39–40 (Darby Translation)

We the church have seen the Messiah more clearly, and we know who he is through the Word of God and the witness of the Holy Spirit. Although we are saved by grace through faith, we are expected to continue in the faith and be committed to Christ up until either the day we pass on or the day of the catching away (whichever comes first). As we just read in Hebrews 11:13, it says that the Old Testament saints died in faith, meaning they never stopped believing the Word of the LORD. They were faithful to it; therefore, God is not ashamed of these faithful ones. God is not ashamed to be called their God. One cannot *be in faith* if they are *not faithful* to the Word of God, believing it with the knowledge they have received.

THE AUTHENTIC

The Bible reveals who the body of Christ really is, and many will become very religious when they are told. The authentic from the bogus are those who continue in the faith and do not let their commitment to the bridegroom go out. To back up my not-so-popular statement, we will begin with the Letter of Hebrews to prove what I say. The Letter of Hebrews is full of warnings to the church to continue in the faith and stay committed to the Messiah. But before we go any further, I want to make it clear that continuing in the faith and staying committed to the LORD does not mean we are perfect in all we say and do. We will not be completely perfect until we are fully redeemed. But what it does mean is the grace of God in which we were saved must still *be operating* in our lives up until the day we die physically or the day of the LORD, whichever comes first for us individually.

If the grace of God is not operating in an individual's life, it is not because God chose to take his grace from them. That is not his desire for anyone. But it does mean the individual has chosen *to discard* God's grace for the desires of this world. I want to emphasize the meaning of the term *discards,* which has the description of one throwing away something that *they view as undesirable,* something they do not want anymore. You must have first received the grace of God to have the option or the freedom to discard it. Once we receive God's salvation, he does not force us to keep it. On the other hand, God expects us not to treat his free gift as "an unholy thing" (Hebrews 10:29). I encourage everyone to remember the parable of the virgins, where the foolish virgins thought they were okay, but they had let their lamps go out due to a lack of oil. Because of this unfortunate situation, they missed the coming of the bridegroom and were then shut out forever.

THE NEW COVENANT SPEAKS TO THE NEW CREATION

As said, we will look at certain scriptures beginning with some from Hebrews, and every reader can discern for themselves if what we are discussing is true. I also need to make one more important point, which is that the New Testament is the covenant God has made between him and those who are new creations in Christ Jesus. Some say that this covenant is between God and Jesus, but I am not sure this is an accurate statement, because this covenant is a conditional covenant, not an unconditional one. And Jesus cannot break this covenant, because he can never deny himself or God.

This covenant does have conditions added to it, in which Jesus can never break. I think a better way of saying it is, Jesus is the stipulation (or the condition) of this covenant (agreement) between the Father and the new creation. The conditions for all that God has promised to us in this covenant depends whether or not we stay in faith to Christ Jesus. Staying in faith to Jesus is the terms of this covenant (agreement) between God and the new creation. This covenant it is not an agreement that God has made to the unbeliever, although the unbeliever can hear it and put their faith in the LORD Jesus Christ and thus enter into this covenant. The New Testament is God speaking to those, "He has predestined for adoption as sons through Yeshua [Jesus] the Messiah [Christ] to himself, according to the good pleasure of his desire" (Ephesians 1:5).

Now after all that has been said, I will show from Scripture what I have said about the body of Christ being those (only) who continues in the faith. Those who continue in the faith are those whom the bridegroom comes for on the day of the catching away. The reason why I say these things, which likely sounds like heresy to many of the religious, is because God wants no one to be deceived.

WE NEED TO PAY ATTENTION
Let us look at what Hebrews chapter two has to say:

> Therefore, we ought to pay greater attention to the things that were heard, lest perhaps we drift away. For if the Word spoken through angels proved steadfast, and every trans-

gression and disobedience received a just recompense; how will we escape if we neglect so great a salvation--which at the first having been spoken through the LORD, was confirmed to us by those who heard; God also bearing witness with them, both by signs and wonders, and by various works of power, and by gifts of the Ruach [Holy] HaKodesh [Spirit], according to his own will?

Hebrew 2:1–4

The Hebrew writer says, "Therefore we ought to pay greater attention (emphasis on greater) to the things that were heard" (Hebrews 2:1a), which refers to the things spoken to us by Jesus (see Hebrews 1:2), who is the *Word* of God. It also says in Hebrews chapter twelve, "See that you don't refuse him who speaks. For if they didn't escape when they refused him who warned on the Eretz [Earth], how much more will we not escape who turn away from him who warns from heaven" (Hebrews 12:25). In verse one it says we need to pay greater attention to the Word, "lest perhaps we drift away" (Hebrews 2:1b). Drift away from what? Drift away from the salvation we have received because of our negligence. Some may argue and say this is referring to the unbeliever not paying attention to the gospel message to receive salvation. I disagree with this belief because the writer uses the personal pronoun "we," which refers to the believers, including the writer of Hebrews himself. No one can be a believer unless they first receive God's free gift of salvation by grace through faith in the LORD Jesus Christ.

In this passage from the second chapter of Hebrews the *believer* is asked this question: "How will we escape if we neglect so great a salvation?" (Hebrews 2:3a). This salvation that begins by putting faith in Christ's death and resurrection was first spoken by Jesus and confirmed by the disciples. It also came with the witness of the Father through signs, wonders, miracles, and gifts of the Spirit of God. With all this evidence, there is still the danger of those who drift away from the faith because they neglect the gift of salvation, which they have received freely. To be negligent of this great salvation we have received is to step, or walk, on the Son of God and to consider the blood of the covenant with which we were sanctified as an unholy thing (see Hebrews 10:29). This verse also adds that these actions insult the *spirit of grace*. If one who calls themselves a believer does not neglect God's great salvation, there is no danger of them drifting away. To maintain God's great salvation, the receiver of it must put their trust in the giver of it wholeheartedly, especially when they are tempted to go their own way. It says in verse eighteen of chapter two, "For in that he himself has suffered being tempted, he is able to help those who are tempted" (Hebrews 2:18).

This is not the time to be walking in deception, my brothers and sisters, for whatever we sow, we will also reap. It says in Galatians chapter six:

> Don't be deceived. God is not mocked, for whatever man sows, that will he also reap. For he who sows to his own flesh will from the flesh reap corruption. But he who sows to the Spirit will from the Spirit reap eternal life.
>
> Galatians 6:7–8

If you are one of the people who believe that this passage means if you sow to the flesh, you will receive corruption in the flesh only, then you better seek for understanding before it is too late. Yes, you will reap corruption in your flesh also. For example, if you involve yourself in sexual immorality, you may reap disease; but the corruption being referred to here is the *opposite* of eternal life.

The intention of this topic, my friend, is not to set you off in fear, but, for your sake, to set you off in the direction of the LORD. To keep you from *neglecting this great salvation* we have received by grace. As we have been discussing, it is only those who continue in the faith by which we have been called who will not drift away from the LORD's great salvation. If anyone chooses to stick to doctrine that teaches otherwise, then there is the high possibility you can slip away from the grace, mercy, and peace of God.

LET GOD DO HIS GOOD WORK

Our good works were not good enough to earn this salvation, but when we heard the Word and made the confession that Jesus is LORD and believed in our spirit that God lifted him up from the dead, we then received this great salvation. This began the salvation process in our lives in which Paul said: "Being confident of this very thing, that he who began a good work in you will complete it until the day of Yeshua [Jesus] the Messiah [Christ]" (Philippians 1:6). This means that from the day we received Christ, God works in us to finish his work of salvation, right up till the coming of the LORD. From the day we received God's salvation until the day we are fully redeemed, we have the responsibility to continue in the faith, which is complete commitment to the LORD Jesus Christ. This allows God to complete his work in us.

God does not twist our arms to keep us in submission to his will, but we must be willing to submit. I hope I am making it absolutely clear that I believe fully in the grace of God and that I am in full agreement of Jesus's power to keep us. When a person departs from faith in Jesus Christ, it does not mean that Christ's power is not sufficient enough to keep them, because it is; but it does mean that the individual who departs *did not let* Christ's power keep them. We see that Paul writes in this vein: "But the Spirit says expressly that in later times some will fall away from the faith, paying attention to seducing spirits and doctrines of demons" (1Timothy 4:1). This is a prophetic Word given by the Holy Spirit through Paul, pertaining to the spiritual condition of some Christians in the time we are living today. This is the time just prior to the end of the church age, when the door will be shut. This group that falls away from the faith could be considered as being among the foolish virgins.

Hebrews chapter three gives plenty of warning concerning this great salvation we have received, which is by grace through faith. I encourage you to read Hebrews chapter three and listen to what the Spirit of God is saying before you go any further. When you believe the Spirit has helped make chapter three clear to you, turn to chapter thirteen.

Do Not Be Shut Out!

Now that you have read through Hebrews chapter three, can you see what the Holy Spirit is trying to communicate? It is so important that we listen to him. The sons and daughters of God cannot be led by the Holy Spirit unless we listen to every word he has to say. The things the Holy Spirit has to say are for our benefit so that we do not drift away from the faith in which we have been called.

God's House

The Spirit of God, through the writer of Hebrews, compares Jesus to Moses in Hebrews 3:1–6. Concerning Moses, it says in verse five: "Moshe [Moses] indeed was faithful in his (God's) entire house as a servant, for a testimony of those things which were afterward to be spoken" (Hebrews 3:5). Moses was a faithful servant in God's entire house, the house God built, which refers to God's people. We will not find anyone else of Moses's contemporaries who were more faithful to God than he was. Moses's faithfulness in God's entire house was an example of the life he lived, so much so that it would be talked about as time went on.

Concerning our LORD, it says, "But Messiah is faithful as a Son over his house, whose house we are, if we hold fast our confidence and the glorying of our hope firm to the end." (Hebrews 3:6). Moses was a faithful servant *in* God's entire house, but Jesus is faithful *over* the entire house. We see in this passage that Jesus has received more honor than Moses, because in fact Jesus is the builder of God's house, in whose house we who believe are. The church is God's house, built on the foundation of the apostles and prophets, with our LORD Jesus being the Chief Cornerstone. Moses was in all likelihood the greatest servant ever in the household of God, but Jesus is the head over the entire household, meaning he has even authority over faithful Moses.

Now notice what the second part of verse six says. It says, "Whose house we are, if we hold fast our confidence and the glorying of our hope firm to the end" (Hebrews 3:6bc). Those in the church are God's house *only if we continue firmly in the faith until the end,* which refers to the day of the catching away or until the end of one's physical life. Again, do not be confused by whom the writer of Hebrews is referring to in this passage. In verse one it tells us it is we, the church, who share in the heavenly calling: "Therefore, holy brothers, partakers of a heavenly calling" (Hebrews 3:1a). The writer of this letter is making it very clear that God only considers those who *hold fast to Jesus firm to the end* of our physical life as his house, because Jesus is our confidence and hope. Jesus is our confidence and our hope because he has been appointed head over God's entire household. It says in Ephesians, "And put all [things] under his feet, and gave him [to be] the head over all [things] to the church" (Ephesians 1:22, Webster's Bible). Back to verse one; it says we are to "consider the Apostle and Kohen Gadol [High Priest] of our confession" (Hebrews 3:1b), who is, of course, our LORD Jesus, meaning we are to keep our mind on him. We who are the household of God are to focus our mind and our attention on him constantly, firmly, until the end, because Christ is our confidence and our hope.

As we continue to look at Hebrews chapter three, we see how to hold fast our confidence and the glory of our hope, from verses seven to nineteen. Ever since the process of salvation has begun in my life, I have heard this portion of scripture to refer only to the sinner—those who have not been made righteous; but as we listen to the Spirit, we see this passage is for those who have been made righteous. From Hebrews 3:7–11, we see the writer of this letter say the Holy Spirit is speaking. Of course, we all understand it is the Holy Spirit who has authored all the scripture, but here the writer is emphasizing this point. This passage is taken from Psalms ninety-five to reveal to the partakers of the heavenly calling what the result will be of an evil heart of unbelief.

A HEART GONE HARD

The Spirit reminds us in our passage of study that Israel tested the patience of the LORD when they were going through the trial in the wilderness. Israel *hardened their hearts* and rebelled against the LORD, which caused the LORD to be angry with them. The Greek word used here for *angry* has a harsher connotation than the term *grieved,* as some translations use. In fact, the Greek word the writer of Hebrews uses expresses the idea that God was filled with wrath or that he was extremely angry with his people. What added to God's anger was that Israel saw the mighty works of God for forty years, and they still had hearts that lacked faith. God said about them: "Always do they go astray in heart, and these have not known my ways" (Hebrews 3:10b, Young's Literal Translation). So God promised himself that this group who go astray will never enter into his rest (see Hebrews 3:11).

Then the Hebrew writer tells us, "Beware, brothers, lest perhaps there be in any one of you an evil heart of unbelief, in falling away from the living God" (Hebrews 3:12). Yes, the writer is writing directly to his *holy brothers*, who are partakers of the *heavenly calling*. Someone may ask the question, "How can someone who has been made a new creation in Christ Jesus have an evil heart of unbelief?" Unbelief is produced from a lack of faith, which can taint even a pure spirit. The term *heart* in this statement refers to the person's *spirit*, not their physical heart. The term *taint* means *to become blemished*. Some people will certainly disagree with me (I know the different theologies) that the born-again spirit can become tainted or blemished; but I will have to ask these people, "Then how can a brother (a person who is born-again, as this verse says) go back again to 'an evil heart of unbelief' (Hebrews 3:12b), as the author of Hebrews gives warning?"

I will also ask, "Why did the apostle Paul say for the beloved (those born-again) to cleanse their spirit from defilement in 2 Corinthians?" "Having therefore these promises, beloved, let us cleanse ourselves from all defilement of flesh and spirit, perfecting holiness in the fear of God" (2 Corinthians 7:1). (Cleansing oneself from defilement of flesh and spirit means one must appropriate the forgiveness of God. See 1 John 1:9). The lack of faith the writer of Hebrews is referring to is in Jesus the Apostle and High Priest of our confession. We confessed him as LORD initially to become partakers of the heavenly calling, but as time goes on some begin to not (and I strongly emphasis the word *not*) hold fast their confidence in Christ Jesus. This sometimes happens during the day of trial when some hearts turn to unbelief, or in other words, their spirit begins to fall away from the living God. Many times this happens because the person desires the world more than they do the kingdom of heaven. The apostle John writes, "Don't love the world, neither the things that are in the world. If anyone loves the world, the Father's love isn't in him" (1 John 2:15).

THE RESULT OF NEGLECT

The spirit of a man is what God initially redeems when he or she receives salvation. Remember, we discussed this earlier in chapter eleven (*No Oil*) that when a person gets born-again, God recreates the person's spirit into a sinless spirit in which he removes their sin, just as if they had never sinned. But the problem arises when a born-again person abuses *their* recreated spirit. What I mean by this is they don't obey the LORD and renew their mind, as we are commanded to do. "Don't be conformed to this world, but be transformed by the renewing of your mind, so that you may prove what is the good, and acceptable, and perfect will of God" (Romans 12:2). When we do not renew our mind to the Word of God, it hinders God's transforming process in our life because our mind is then conformed to the world, instead of God's will. We also neglect to offer our body as a living sacrifice, as Paul encourages us: "Therefore I urge you, brothers, by the mercies of God, to present your bodies a living sacrifice, holy, acceptable to God, which is your spiritual service" (Romans 12:1). The neglect of these things brings direct abuse to our recreated spirit. It says in Proverbs, "Keep your heart (your spirit) with all diligence, for out of it is the wellspring of life" (Proverbs 4:23). The born-again person must guard their spirit (heart) so they do not re-contaminate it with the things from the old sinful nature. We have been made in the righteousness of God through faith in Jesus Christ, but we have to stay in God's righteousness by replenishing our faith in Jesus Christ and trusting in his blood.

FAITH NEEDS NOURISHMENT

The faith we had to receive salvation is not enough to sustain us throughout our entire transformation period, unless a person is like the thief on the cross who went to Paradise his very first day (I hope you get my meaning right away). When a person puts faith in Jesus Christ to receive salvation and then lives for a significant amount of time, they are going to come to a point in time when they need their faith replenished. One important function of faith is to get us through to the next trial we face. It says in James:

> Count it all joy, my brothers, when you fall into various temptations, knowing that the testing of your faith produces patience. Let patience have its perfect work, that you may be perfect and complete, lacking in nothing.
>
> James 1:2–4

As we grow in faith, our faith needs to become stronger to get us through each trial, because it is during the times of trial that our faith can diminish, as did Israel in the wilderness and they hardened their spirit. Anyone who has lived for any length of time knows that trials do come. They also know what I am trying to express here. Our faith in the LORD has been manufactured to grow, as we can see here:

Not boasting beyond proper limits in other men's labors, but having hope that as your faith grows, we will be abundantly enlarged by you in our sphere of influence.

2 Corinthians 10:15

We are bound to always give thanks to God for you, brothers, even as it is appropriate, because your faith grows exceedingly, and the love of each and every one of you towards one another abounds.

2 Thessalonians 1:3

What I am saying is if we are not growing in faith than we are shrinking back, and the LORD is not pleased with those who shrink back in faith: "But the righteous will live by faith. If he shrinks back, my soul has no pleasure in him" (Hebrews 10:38).

WE ARE DEAD TO SIN (SUPPOSED TO BE, ANYWAY)

When our spirit was recreated, we died to sin, according to Romans 6:2, so we cannot (more like, *should* not) live in sin any longer, but we all know that many who have received salvation carry on with many of their sins. For a lack of better words, they still live an ungodly life. Most of us have been guilty of this, even though the Bible says we have been crucified with Christ and our old sinful nature *is supposed to* be done away with. Paul taught us that "Our old man was crucified with him [Christ] that the body of sin might be done away with, so that we would no longer be in bondage to sin" (Romans 6:6). We are to consider ourselves *finished with sin* and live only for the one who carried our sins. We read: "Thus also consider yourselves also to be dead to sin, but alive to God in Messiah [Christ] Yeshua [Jesus] our LORD. Therefore don't let sin reign in your mortal body, that you should obey it in its lusts" (Romans 6:11–12). If this were not possible for us to do when it actually has already been done in us by the power of God, then why did Paul say this is what we must do? Does anyone think Paul is being too harsh on us with these commands? I would, if I desired to live to my old, sinful nature (but I do not), think he is being too strict with us. Just like a nineteenth century schoolmarm with a very hard yardstick. How could we walk in freedom and know we have been set free from the power of sin if Paul did not teach us these things?

If God is working in us, then it is possible to live for Christ and sin shall have no dominion over us; but let us stop making excuses. Sometimes we do make excuses, and we have the tendency to call our sins weaknesses to make it not sound so bad. But nonetheless, God has made a way for us when we do sin or we fall short of his glory by confessing our sin: "If we confess our sins, he is faithful and righteous to forgive us the sins, and to cleanse us from all unrighteousness" (1 John 1:9).

FOLLOW THE PLAN

When we neglect the procedures God has provided for us—by this I mean confessing our sin—it leads us into the place of falling away. Falling away begins by the *resurgence* of an evil heart of unbelief like we had before we were made new creations, instead of a heart of faith. This parallels the believer with the foolish virgin who did not have enough oil to keep her lamp from going out. Falling away from the living God is a process that takes a substantial period of time to become full blown. The power of Jesus's blood is strong, but when a person begins to treat "the blood of the covenant" as "an unholy thing" (Hebrews 10:29c), that person's *conscious choice* begins to diminish the *effectiveness* of Christ's blood in their life. Thus, a falling away from the living God begins to occur due to an evil heart of unbelief.

The heart of unbelief is referred to as "evil" because "whatever is not of faith is sin" (Romans 14:23). It is the deceitfulness of sin that begins to harden the heart, which produces unbelief instead of faith. Believers are to encourage each other, day after day, to stay with the LORD: "But exhort one another day by day, so long as it is called "today;" lest any one of you be hardened by the deceitfulness of sin" (Hebrews 3:13). We do not want to be like the foolish virgins who let their lamps go out because they did not have enough oil to keep them going. Then when the bridegroom came, they were off looking for more oil, and, to their loss, the door was shut on them, and they were then refused entry. The foolish virgin is a picture of the one who receives salvation and does not hold firmly their confidence until the end, as it says in Hebrews: "For we have become partakers of Messiah [Christ], if we hold fast the beginning of our confidence firm to the end" (Hebrews 3:14).

DO NOT BE DECEIVED: PLEASE!

The writer of Hebrews is making every effort in chapter three to make sure the one who receives Christ is not deceived. He reveals to us that the Israelites who disobeyed in the wilderness did not enter God's rest because of their unbelief. So it is with those who put their faith in Christ at the beginning of their salvation experience. If they do not hold fast to their confidence, or assurance, until the end, they will not remain partakers of Christ. The phrase "until the end" refers to the end of the church age, which is the end of our salvation process when our physical bodies are finally redeemed.

Someone may say that Israel was under the law, and we are under grace. God functioned in grace with Israel also, as he functions in grace with us. The law just made them more con-science of their sin, so they would turn to God. Of course, they did not have it as easy as we do, because the Lamb of God still had to come to remove their sin completely, like he has done for us. But if they would have followed the procedures that God laid out before them, which was to follow the *rules of atonement* (in the Torah) and to do as God said: "It shall happen, if you shall listen diligently to my mitzvoth [commands] which I command you this day, to love the LORD your God, and to serve him with all your heart and with all your soul" (Deuteronomy 11:13), they could have lasted until the Lamb of God came. (No one can say that this was not a form of grace that God functioned in with his people, Israel.) But again, most of Israel chose to function in a spirit of unbelief, which is why God said, "I was displeased with that generation," and "They always err in their heart, but they didn't know my ways'" (Hebrews 3:10). That is why we Chris-tians have a *greater responsibility* to live free and not carelessly, because of the blood Jesus spilt for us. Some of the church has the idea God's grace allows them to live in sin, and they will automatically be forgiven. Read what Paul says here in Romans: "What shall we say then? Shall we continue in sin, that grace may abound? May it never be! We who died to sin, how could we live in it any longer?" (Romans 6:1–2).

DON'T BE A DOG: OR A SOW

We will continue to look on this topic even further in the next chapter so there will be no doubt what we are learning. We will stay in the Letter of Hebrews a little more, and then we will look at some of what the apostle Paul taught about the believer staying in the faith. The reason why I am sticking on this topic is so the Holy Spirit can reveal to us how important it is not to turn from the way of righteousness, which was freely given to us by the grace of God through the blood of Jesus Christ our LORD. The apostle Peter, inspired by the Spirit of God, wrote this:

> For if, after they have escaped the defilement of the world through the knowledge of the LORD and Savior Yeshua [Jesus] the Messiah [Christ], they are again entangled therein and overcome, the last state has become worse with them than the first. For it would be better for them not to have known the way of righteousness, than, after knowing it, to turn back from the holy mitzvah [commandment] delivered to them. But it has happened to them according to the true proverb, "The dog turns to his own vomit again" and "the sow that had washed to wallowing in the mire."
>
> 2 Peter 2:20–22

WE HAVE A RESPONSIBILITY

The catching away of the church is too near for any of us who have become partakers of the heavenly calling to think that just because we have received the gift of salvation we will automatically be part of this glorious event. I know that this has been taught as long as I have received salvation, back in 1985. But this is not what the Bible teaches us. The New Testament teaches us that God has made us responsible to conform to his will, and it is his will that we complete the salvation process and be fully redeemed. God's will is not automatically done; we have to come into agreement with it. We may receive the gift of salvation, but then we must conform to God's will pertaining to salvation.

He has given us the start by removing sin from our spirit when we first believed and recreating our spirit like Adam's when he was first created. Our LORD has given us his Spirit to teach us how to work the Word in our life so our mind can be renewed so we can conform to God's will. God has given us his power so we can live the new life, which he has freely given us. God expects us to work with him as he works in us—his desire for us.

> So then, my beloved, even as you have always obeyed, not only in my presence, but now much more in my absence, work out your own salvation with fear and trembling. For it is God who works in you both to will and to work, for his good pleasure.
>
> Philippians 2:12–13

We have to work with the Spirit of God and not against him. Am I saying that if we do not work with God and work out our salvation he takes his gift of salvation back? No! But what I am saying is if we do not work with the Spirit but against him, we dishonor this free gift and treat Christ's blood as an unholy thing (see Hebrews 10:29). As I said before, this insults the spirit of grace. Working out our salvation means we let the Spirit work in us, and we work with him, letting him do everything he needs to do.

If we hold fast our confidence and the glorying of our hope firm to the end of our physical life or the catching away, whichever comes first, then yes, we will be changed in the twinkling of an eye and receive our promised glorified spiritual bodies. Again, I must make it clear that the Bible does not teach that we will be perfect in all we say and all we do while in these earthly bodies. That is why God has made the way for his grace to continue in our life through confessing our sins (see 1 John 1:9). But we are to keep our eyes on Jesus and not ourselves or the world.

Make Sure the Door Is Open: Learn Obedience

Jesus Christ is our great High Priest, who has much understanding in how weak we can sometimes be. When he was on this earth in his physical body, he was tempted in so many ways that he knows what a person goes through. Praise to his holy name that even though he was tempted, he never sinned. This is why we need to hold fast to the faith we confess in him as it says in Hebrews:

> Having then a great Kohen Gadol [High Priest], who has passed through the heavens, Yeshua [Jesus], the Son of God, let us hold tightly to our confession. For we don't have a Kohen Gadol [High Priest] who can't be touched with the feeling of our infirmities, but one who has been in all points tempted like we are, yet without sin.
>
> Hebrews 4:14–15

If we find ourselves beginning to slip away from Christ, we can then go to God with confidence, knowing he will not turn us away, and we can receive his mercy and find his grace to sustain us: "Let us therefore draw near with boldness to the throne of grace, that we may receive mercy, and may find grace for help in time of need" (Hebrews 4:16).

When Jesus was on the earth as a flesh-and-blood man, he knew he would be put on the cross and receive the sin of the whole world upon himself. Although he never sinned, he would become sin for us: "For him who knew no sin he made to be sin on our behalf; so that in him we might become the righteousness of God" (2 Corinthians 5:21). The consequences for Jesus would be that he would have to die not only physically but also spiritually. His spirit would have to suffer eternal death because of you and me so our spirit (and soul and body) may receive eternal life. This is why when Jesus was in the flesh, he prayed fervently to his Father, who could save him from this death, as the writer of Hebrews stated. "He, in the days of his flesh, having offered up prayers and petitions with strong crying and tears to him who was able to save him from death, and having been heard for his godly fear" (Hebrews 5:7). His Father heard his prayers and petitions because Jesus submitted his will to his Father. "Though he was a Son, yet learned obedience by the things which he suffered" (Hebrews 5:8).

JESUS LEARNED OBEDIENCE

Jesus had to *learn obedience* to the will of the Father over his own will. Was Jesus's will not naturally lined up with the Father's will all his natural life? Yes, it was, but Jesus did have his challenges. We know that this sacrifice was not an easy thing for Jesus as he made this passionate plea to his Father: "Abba, Father, all things are possible to you. Please remove this cup from me. However, not what I desire, but what you desire" (Mark 14:36). Jesus knew he was the Lamb of God, and he knew that with this calling came a horrible death on the cross.

Jesus knew the writings in Isaiah fifty-three that he would be "As a lamb that is led to the slaughter" (Isaiah 53:7) and "The LORD has laid on him the iniquity of us all" (Isaiah 53:6). Can you imagine what went through the mind of Jesus, not only that night in Gethsemane, but ever since he understood, likely as a child, all that his calling encompassed? All his natural life, Jesus would have had to submit his will to the Father's will, especially having the knowledge that the sins of the world would be put on him. But because he learned to be obedient in his natural body, Jesus's desire was not his own will but his Father's. Thus, Jesus was the perfect Lamb of God, and his Father was able to raise him from eternal and physical death on the third day. Some will say it was Jesus's faith alone that produced this result, but I say that without godly fear that produces *obedience,* there is no faith.

WE MUST LEARN OBEDIENCE

Jesus's spirit, which suffered eternal death for each of us, was made perfect again. I say made perfect *again* because before Jesus became sin he knew no sin, so his spirit was perfect until the sins of the world were put upon him. Then, because the iniquities of us all were laid upon him, Jesus died spiritually. If he did not die spiritually, then he could not receive the judgment that was meant for you and me. Now that Jesus has been made perfect again, he gives eternal completeness to all who obey him. "He became to all of those who obey him the author of eternal salvation" (Hebrews 5:9). What the Christian needs to learn from the passage in Hebrews 5:7–10 is that Jesus is the one where eternal life originates. For the Christian to receive eternal life, we need to *continually obey Christ,* even after we have received spiritual wholeness, just like Jesus obeyed his Father. Obedience to the faith is part of the process of our salvation. It is spiritually impossible to continue in the faith and not be obedient to it.

This may not sit well with you because you are quite possibly "Not experienced in the word of righteousness" (Hebrews 5:13), and you may still be a baby needing milk (see Hebrews 5:12–13). Without any disrespect, you may have received salvation many years ago, but you cannot handle solid food yet. You are having a hard time understanding that salvation is a process, and obedience to the Savior is integral for the transformation to be completed. You may be among the group who were taught that just because you received salvation, no matter how you live, you will be among those who are caught away. If you are, then I bring to your attention again that Jesus "Having been made perfect, became to all of those who obey him the author of eternal salvation" (Hebrews 5:9). No one can continue to have faith in Jesus after receiving him if *obedience* is continually absent.

WHAT IS "ETERNAL" SALVATION?

I want to show you what the writer of Hebrews is referring to when he uses the phrase "eternal salvation" instead of just the term *salvation*. This is the only place in the entire Bible where the term "eternal salvation" is used. In every other place, only the word *salvation* is used. The word *salvation* is used to describe what God has done for us through Christ's death and resurrection, which is deliverance from sin, freedom from the powers of darkness, health, victory, and so on. Everywhere in the New Testament when we see the word *salvation,* it is either referring to Jesus, who brought us salvation, or it refers to what has been given to us when we received the one who brought it to us. But in Hebrews 5:9, the writer uses the word *salvation* in a different context. It is not only used in reference to what God has done for us here in the physical realm, as it refers to everywhere else, but he equates it with receiving our glorified spiritual bodies by attaching it to the word *eternal*. By joining the two words together, the writer of Hebrews is using the phrase "eternal salvation" to describe salvation *after* we receive our glorified spiritual bodies. Eternal salvation literally means salvation in eternity. At that time we, the bride of Christ, will be eternal creatures in spiritual bodies (just like Jesus has), instead of the earthly bodies we possess now.

So the author of Hebrews is revealing that there is salvation in eternity, which commences once we receive our spiritual bodies. The point he is primarily trying to make is that Jesus is "the author of eternal salvation" only to "those who obey him" (see Hebrew 5:9). Eternal salvation is physical salvation complete when our physical body is redeemed. Eternal salvation is our redemption being fully manifest when our physical bodies are changed into spiritual bodies, which happens at the catching away. I hope you are not getting tired of this, but I need to say it again—salvation comes when we receive Christ, which means only our spirit man is delivered from sin and unrighteousness. It has been made complete and it lacks nothing. We are to work this salvation into our souls by renewing our mind with the Word of God so the transformation process can continue into our bodies so we can receive eternal salvation on the day of the catching away. Only those who obey Christ while in their physical bodies will receive eternal salvation. In other words, only those who obey Christ will take part in the catching away and then receive glorified spiritual bodies.

OBEDIENCE IS ESSENTIAL

Brand-new Christians have the advantage over some who have been saved for any length of time because their obedient levels to Christ are very high. But the problem begins to manifest when a person begins on the road of righteousness and let their obedient level begin to diminish; thus their commitment to the LORD begins to go out just like the foolish virgins who let their lamps go out. Some people may say that I am leaving no room for God's grace. But God's grace can only operate in those who practice receiving it. A person who has known the way of righteousness and then gets entangled back into the world and overcome by it again does so because they do not practice walking in the grace of God.

The mature realize that anyone who receives salvation and then does not hold onto it is because of the choices a person makes. Some people will say that no one can receive salvation and then lose it. What is the definition of the word *losing* anyways? First of all, I am not meaning that the person loses salvation because of an unforeseen accident or by mistake. What is meant by a person losing their salvation is they failed to keep it or they let it slip away because they did not see any value in it.

WHAT ABOUT FORGIVENESS: ARE NOT ALL OUR SINS FORGIVEN?

Maybe right now you are thinking that Jesus removed our sins past, present, and future. Yes, he did, my brother and sister, but he did this for the whole world, as it says: "And he is the atoning sacrifice for our sins, and not for ours only, but also for the whole world" (1 John 2:2). Even though Christ *has atoned* for the sins of the whole world, more people have never, and will never, receive salvation and have their spirits recreated like us who are born again, because they deny Jesus Christ. Most of mankind will stand before the LORD at the great white throne judgment because their names will not be found in the Book of Life (see Revelation 20:11–15). A person's name is written in the Book of Life when they become a new creature in Christ Jesus. Their names stay in the Book of Life *if they continue with Christ* and not depart from him.

It says in Revelation 3:5: "He who overcomes will be arrayed in white garments, and I will in no way blot his name out of the book of life, and I will confess his name before my Father, and before his angels" In the previous verse, Jesus said there were a few in the church of Sardis who "did not defile their garments" (Revelation 3:4), which refers to *defiling their righteousness* or their right standing with God. It is those who defile their righteousness who will have their names blotted out of the Book of Life. The grace of God is not weak, my friend, but we have to remain within the bounds of his grace.

SELF-AFFLICTION

We need to continue with this teaching so all will have godly fear just like Christ, who learned obedience by the things he suffered. If Jesus Christ had to learn obedience, then how much more do his followers? This is written in Hebrews chapter six:

> For concerning those who were once enlightened and tasted of the heavenly gift, and were made partakers of the Ruach HaKodesh [Holy Spirit], and tasted the good Word of God, and the powers of the age to come, and then fell away, it is impossible to renew them again to repentance; seeing

they crucify the Son of God for themselves again, and put him to open shame.

Hebrews 6:4–6

It is written that Jesus tasted death for us "that he by the grace of God should taste death for every man" (Hebrews 2:9c, KJV) so that we could taste and experience the "heavenly gift" (Hebrews 6:4a), which results in every Christian being made the righteousness of God and "partakers of the Holy Spirit" (Hebrews 6:4b). If through *continual willful disobedience* one falls away from faith in Jesus Christ, then it is *self-inflicted destruction*. This begs the question, why are we not being taught this by those who have been appointed to feed the household of God, the word of God, that there is the possibility of falling away from Christ by continually intentionally disobeying what he says in his word?

FALLING AWAY

The apostle Paul said, "Let no man deceive you by any means: for [that day shall not come], except there come a falling away first, and that man of sin be revealed, the son of perdition" (2 Thessalonians 2:3, KJV). We see Paul also write to Timothy: "But the Spirit says expressly that in later times some will fall away from the faith, paying attention to seducing spirits and doctrines of demons" (1 Timothy 4:1). Paul is saying that prior to the catching away of the body of Christ, there will be a *falling away* from the faith of Jesus Christ. The writer of Hebrews (whether it be Paul I am not sure) says that for these who fall away "it is impossible to renew them again to repentance" (Hebrews 6:6). The reason for this is because Christ was crucified for them once already, and through their *continual willful disobedience,* they fall away and cannot re-crucify Christ again (see also Hebrews 10:26). Falling away from the faith refers to departing, abandoning, or forsaking Jesus Christ. Jesus was publicly shamed when he was crucified in April, AD 32, so for a person who "was once enlightened and tasted of the heavenly gift, and were made partakers of the Holy Spirit, and tasted the good Word of God, and the powers of the age to come" (Hebrews 6:4–5) to then forsake and abandon Jesus Christ is to literally thumb their nose at him. To thumb your nose at someone means that you disrespect that person.

THE POWER OF CHRIST'S BLOOD

We need to continue to look at some more of what the Holy Spirit inspired the writer of Hebrews so that we will be fully convinced that salvation is a process and cooperate with God and continue in the transformation process by renewing our mind. It says in Philippians, "Work out your own salvation with fear and trembling" (Philippians 2:12c). We cannot do this on our own. "For it is God who works in you both to will and to work, for his good pleasure" (Philippians 2:13). Can you see that God works in us "to will and to work," giving us the responsibility to let God work in us (the salvation he gave to us) so that our will will conform to his will. That is what it means to work out your own salvation. It belongs to us, but he does the work if we let him. I will say it this way: *Our Father works in us by his spirit's power to get us to choose (will) to work out our salvation, which pleases him.*

Next, we come to some very heavy language used by the Holy Spirit in Hebrews chapter ten. But first, I want to encourage you that God prepared the body of Jesus Christ to take away the sins of the world, which the blood of bulls and goats could not do (see Hebrews 10:4–5). Jesus said to the Father, "Behold, I have come to do your will" (Hebrews 10:9a). Then in verse ten it says, "By which will we have been sanctified through the offering of the body of Yeshua [Jesus] the Messiah [Christ] once for all" (Hebrews 10:10). This means that no more sacrifices for sins is needed, for by this one sacrifice, by our Holy High Priest, Jesus, removed our sins forever. In 1 Corinthians chapter six it says, "We were washed. We were sanctified. We were justified in the name of the LORD Yeshua [Jesus], and in the Spirit of our God" (1Corinthians 6:11). The blood of bulls and goats could not do this for us, but the blood of the LORD Jesus Christ washed away our sin. As said before, the power of his blood removed every trace of sin from our spirit and made it as if it had never sinned. This is what it means to be sanctified and why we are referred to as new creations. "Therefore if anyone is in Messiah [Christ], he is a new creation. The old things have passed away. Behold, all things have become new" (2 Corinthians 5:17). This is why we have the opportunity to enter the *most holy place* with boldness because of what our High Priest, the LORD Jesus Christ, has done for us.

This sacrifice of Christ was more than anything anyone could ever do for us. I am so glad that Jesus desired the will of his Father more than the desire of his emotions in the garden of Gethsemane the night prior to his crucifixion. Who can criticize Jesus for the way he felt, considering he knew he would be cut off from his Father while the sins of the world were being poured into him? This is what our LORD prayed: "Abba, Father, all things are possible to you. Please remove this cup from me. However, not what I desire, but what you desire" (Mark 14:36). This is why we must, with all diligence, do as it written. "Let us hold fast the confession of our hope unyieldingly. For he who promised is faithful" (Hebrews 10:23).

Our hope is in the LORD Jesus Christ, whom we have confessed as LORD, along with everything he has done for us. We must do this without wavering one inch, because Jesus is faithful to do and complete all he has promised us if we hold on to what it says. "But Messiah [Christ] is faithful as a Son over his house; whose house we are, if we hold fast our confidence and the glorying of our hope firm to the end" (Hebrews 3:6). Do you see the key phrases in these two verses? "Let us hold fast" (Hebrews 10:23a) and "If we hold fast" (Hebrews 3:6b). These two phrases put the responsibility on us to hold fast to the LORD who is our hope, and we need to hold fast our confidence if we want to stay among his household.

It Is Good to Listen

I said a couple of paragraphs back that we will look at *some very heavy language* used by the Holy Spirit in Hebrews chapter ten. This passage is in Hebrews 10:26–31, which I encourage you to study with a sincere heart and a desire to know the truth. Remember this passage is from the Holy Spirit and is not just the personal thought of the writer of Hebrews. I am likely right in saying that many Christians have never heard this passage in any sermon they have heard preached in their church. If you have had this passage taught and preached to you (correctly, I hope) or any of the passages on this topic we have discussed, then your shepherd (pastor and teacher) is preparing you to receive your salvation complete. His desire is to make sure your commitment to the LORD never diminishes.

Many Christians, especially in this end-time generation, just want to hear all the verses from God's Word that are pleasant to their ear. Sometimes the things we desire from the LORD only have an earthly component to it. This is why so many are deceived within their position in the body of Christ. They think they are standing right in the LORD because the Word says by grace we do, but in their heart they are slowly departing from the grace by which they were saved. Just like the foolish virgins who thought their lamps would not go out, many Christians are letting their commitment to the LORD Jesus Christ deteriorate day after day.

I am finally going to give you now Hebrews 10:26–31, which I consider being very heavy language, but I am not going to give you any commentary with it. I do encourage everyone who has received God's salvation to truly let the Holy Spirit teach you the meaning of this passage. Take into consideration all the verses I have given you from the letter of Hebrews and also the specific passages from the letters of Peter and Paul that we have looked at over these last few chapters.

The Holy Spirit says this to everyone who has received salvation by grace through faith:

> For if we sin willfully after we have received the knowledge of the truth, there remains no more a sacrifice for sins, but a certain fearful expectation of judgment, and a fierceness of fire which will devour the adversaries. A man who disregards Moshe's [Moses'] law dies without compassion on the word of two or three witnesses. How much worse punishment, do you think, will he be judged worthy of, who has trodden under foot the Son of God, and has counted the blood of the covenant with which he was sanctified an unholy thing, and has insulted the Spirit of grace? For we know him who said, "Vengeance belongs to me," says the LORD, "I will repay." Again, "The LORD will judge his

people." It is a fearful thing to fall into the hands of the living God.

Hebrews 10:26–31

Now, did you read this passage very carefully? Do you see why I am reluctant to give you my commentary on this passage? I truly believe the Holy Spirit himself prefers to speak to you personally who have tasted the Word of God and the powers of God's kingdom, have been enlightened, have tasted of the heavenly gift of salvation, and who are partakers of the Holy Spirit and power. The day and the hour of the catching away is sooner than we think, so we need to be watching and be ready for the coming of the Son of Man, as Jesus says: "Watch therefore, for you don't know the day nor the hour in which the Son of Man is coming" (Matthew 25:13).

BE A WISE VIRGIN

Paul strongly urges the many that have received the gospel message and have therefore received salvation to *hold firmly* onto it. Now why would the apostle need to warn people to continue in the faith if there was no chance of a person falling from faith in Jesus Christ? Because, as we have been discussing, there is the possibility of drifting away if one does not hold onto the Word of God. Paul says this in 1 Corinthians:

> Now I declare to you, brothers, the Good News which I preached to you, which also you received, in which you also stand, by which also you are saved, if you hold firmly the word which I preached to you—unless you believed in vain.
>
> 1 Corinthians 15:1–2

If we do not hold firmly to the Word of God, then our believing has been unsuccessful. I did not say the Word of God has been unsuccessful, but *our faith* in the Word has been a failure. Paul makes this statement because the Holy Spirit warns us through Paul to stay committed to Jesus Christ and not let our lamps (or rather, our commitment to the Messiah) go out.

Hold on to Him

No matter how difficult life may get or how discouraging things may seem to be, we must *hold onto our faith* in the Lord Jesus Christ and never throw it away. We must always put our Messiah first with full acknowledgment and endure until the day he comes for us, because Paul gives this strong warning:

> This saying is faithful: For if we died with him, we will also live with him. If we endure, we will also reign with him. If we deny him, he also will deny us. If we are faithless, he remains faithful. He can't deny himself.
>
> 2 Timothy 2:11–13

Now make sure you read this passage carefully and listen to what the Spirit of God is saying. We have died in our spirit to the sinful nature when we became new creations; this is what it means to be crucified with Christ. Now the life we live in our natural body, we must live by faith in the Son of God, who loved us and gave himself for us (see Galatians 2:20). We have the *opportunity* to live with him if we die with him.

We must endure or suffer with Christ, which means we must follow him no matter what happens to us, and the result will be that we will reign with him forever. Some teachers don't tell us the whole story when they teach who the church is in Christ Jesus. Yes, they tell us that we are heirs of God, and yes, they tell us that we are joint-heirs with Jesus. But they forget to include "if indeed we suffer with him" (Romans 8:17). This is neglecting *a very important component part* of what it is to be an heir with our Lord. Can you see that the Apostle Paul is teaching that there is *a condition* to being an heir of God and a joint-heir with our Lord? The condition is "if indeed we suffer with him"

(Romans 8:17). We are to be "partakers of Messiah's [Christ's] sufferings" (1 Peter 4:13), meaning we *endure* the persecutions, the insults, the heartaches, and whatever else. If we endure like he endured, we will also reign with Christ now and forever. But on the counter side, if we *deny Christ,* which is not acknowledging him when confronted by men or even our thoughts; then Jesus Christ will *deny or refuse* to acknowledge those who deny him. The LORD Jesus Christ spoke these very important words: "But whoever denies me before men, him I will also deny before my Father who is in heaven" (Matthew 10:33).

We need to hold tightly to our confession of faith in our Great High Priest. If we lose our faith in Christ, which is literally *betraying* him like Judas Iscariot did, Christ remains faithful, which means he stays true to himself, but he will deny those who deny him. Some seem to think if we become faithless, which is literally being unfaithful, that Jesus Christ picks up the slack and remains faithful to keep the unfaithful. But that is not what Paul said to Timothy. "If we deny him, he also will deny us" (2 Timothy 2:12). Rather as said, Christ remains faithful to himself because Jesus cannot deny himself, for he knows who he is in his Father. Jesus Christ is in his Father, and his Father is in him, for they are one in each other (see John 10:30).

Every person who makes the claim that they are a Christian must make sure they stay *committed* to the LORD Jesus Christ and not just to some organization or fellowship that uses Christ's name as a banner. Everyone who has received God's free gift of salvation by faith must continue in the faith and not let their commitment to Jesus go out. To reiterate, we are expected by the Word of the LORD to *continue in the faith* and *be committed* to Christ up until the day of the LORD. We have experienced a spiritual conversion by the power of the gospel; therefore, God's righteousness has been revealed in all who have received salvation so we cannot let ourselves be entangled by the defilement of the world again. If this happens to anyone, then it proves the proverb true that Peter quoted. "But it has happened to them according to the true proverb, 'The dog turns to his own vomit again,' and 'the sow that had washed to wallowing in the mire'" (2 Peter 2:22).

We must abide in Christ so that the Father can prune us so we bear more fruit (see John 15:1–3). The LORD Jesus Christ said this:

> Remain in me, and I in you. As the branch can't bear fruit by itself, unless it remains in the vine, so neither can you, unless you remain in me. I am the vine. You are the branches. He who remains in me, and I in him, the same bears much fruit, for apart from me you can do nothing. If a man doesn't remain in me, he is thrown out as a branch, and is withered; and they gather them, throw them into the fire, and they are burned.
>
> John 15:4–6

So rather than turning back to the sin we were delivered from, we must remain attached to the vine (Jesus) so our Father can prune us so we bear more fruit. Remember, a vine only produces fruit that resembles itself.

DON'T BE A QUITTER

I hope by now, through the Word I have presented, that you can see that Christians can fall away from the faith and therefore will not receive eternal salvation at the day of the catching away, which is sooner than we think. The reason for this information is because God, who has freely given his salvation to all who put their faith in his Son, desires that each recipient of his free gift follow through with their commitment to him. Remaining in the vine (Jesus) is being committed to him. Like I have stated, Christians fall away from the faith not because of a lack of God's grace or because the power of Christ is insufficient but because a person just quits on the LORD, thereby breaking their commitment to him. It is like people who quit in a marriage. A wise saying is that it takes two people to keep a marriage together, but unfortunately, when one person quits, the marriage is usually over. This is exactly what it is like when one gives up on Jesus and the Word of God—the marriage is over.

We must keep our relationship alive with our LORD every day. We must stay committed to him, because he gave us this directive: "Watch therefore, for you don't know the day or the hour in which the Son of Man is coming" (Matthew 25:13). We are so close to receiving our complete redemption that it is foolish to be slumbering. The foolish virgins were not watching for their betrothed one to come with any seriousness at all, or they would have made sure they had enough oil to keep their lamps from going out. Have any of us let our faith in Christ begin to slip, thus allowing his Word to diminish in our heart? If we have, then we are like the foolish ones who had the door shut on them and then were denied access to the marriage feast. If any are in this situation, the Holy Spirit makes this plea:

> For we have become partakers of Messiah [Christ], if we hold fast the beginning of our confidence firm to the end: while it is said, "Today if you will hear his voice, Don't harden your hearts, as in the rebellion.
>
> Hebrews 3:14–15

Beware, brothers, lest perhaps there be in any one of you an evil heart of unbelief, in falling away from the living God.

Hebrews 3:12

THE FAITHFUL AND WISE SERVANT: FEED THE HOUSEHOLD

Those who are called by the LORD to feed his people the right food in its proper season must begin to do so. It is hard to imagine that the catching away is so near, especially to those who have not understood this mystery up until now. But now that we have a greater understanding of how close we are to the coming of the LORD, it would be very foolish to deny the plan of God. For those who choose to continue to still deny how close we are to the catching away, look to God and tell him you do not believe it and why.

Every apostle, prophet, evangelist, pastor, and teacher must make the theme of their messages be about the catching away. When we preach to the unsaved, the focus is on Jesus and his coming again. People need to be saved right now, because the Son of Man is coming literally at any hour. When we teach how the church is supposed to live, the main point must be that the Son of Man is coming at an hour that is sooner than we think. Do not worry about the mockers who follow their fleshly desires and ignorantly say, "Where is the promise of his coming?" (2 Peter 3:4a). We must make sure we feed the household of God their food so they can be anticipating the LORD's coming every day. We need to teach those who have received salvation to obey the Word of God, doing as it says and living as it says to the extent of our knowledge of it. And as I said before, if any minister of the kingdom has no knowledge of what food they should be feeding the household of God in this generation, then maybe *today* is a good day to start getting some.

The Purified Mind

The hope of the Lord's coming purifies the mind of the one who has received the word of truth, as the apostle John said:

> Beloved, now we are children of God, and it is not yet revealed what we will be. But we know that, when he is revealed, we will be like him; for we will see him just as he is. Everyone who has this hope set on him purifies himself, even as he is pure.
>
> 1 John 3:2–3

When the household of God purifies themselves, they are participating in their salvation process by working out their salvation and are literally watching and getting ready for the hour of the Lord.

The household of God is being robbed of the crown of righteousness, which is a special crown that will be handed out to those who have kept the faith, like Paul (see 2 Timothy 4:7), and have loved the Lord's appearing. Paul said this:

> From now on, there is stored up for me the crown of righteousness, which the Lord, the righteous judge, will give to me on that day; and not to me only, but also to all those who have loved his appearing.
>
> 2 Timothy 4:8

Those who are looking forward with a heartfelt desire to the coming of the Lord will receive with Paul on the day of the catching away this special crown. The reason I say the household of God is being robbed is because those called to feed the house are not doing so. How can the house know about the catching away unless they are being fed this important information? But let us not lay all the blame on the teachers and pastors of the house of the Living God! Each will have to give an account of their life before God. We too can search the Word of God, and the Holy Spirit will teach us. The important thing, especially right now, is to not deny the LORD's coming is close. His Word says it is close. Can we see it? Do we believe it? Or are we like the blind leaders of Israel's past, who could not even discern the day when Jesus came the first time?

THE DAY AND THE HOUR: IS SOONER THAN WE THINK

Are we watching? Are we ready? Or are we like the foolish virgins who took no oil with them for their lamps and therefore had the door to the marriage feast shut on them? Are we feeding on the proper diet for these last times, which will make us spiritually healthy and strong? If we are feeding on the right food, then we will not deny this is the due season, and therefore, we will be watching and ready for the hour of our betrothed's coming, just like the wise virgin. If we are wise virgins, then we will never hear the words that the bridegroom said to the foolish virgins, which were, "'Most assuredly I tell you, I don't know you'" (Matthew 25:12).

We must stay focused on Jesus and never stray away from him. We must wage the good warfare, as Paul said:

> This charge I commit to you, my child Timothy, according to the prophecies which led the way to you, that by them

you may wage the good warfare; holding faith and a good conscience; which some having thrust away made a shipwreck concerning the faith.

1 Timothy1:18–19

In chapter sixteen, I show each passage that pertains to the catching away. Along with each passage I have written some commentary so you can see how vitally important it is to be watching and ready for this glorious event. I pray the grace, mercy, and peace of our God is with each of you. Amen.

The Catching Away: References

The Day and the Hour has been presented to reveal how close we are to the day of the catching away. It has also revealed very important information to who will be partakers in this supernatural transition from the physical to the spiritual. To close off this book, it is now appropriate to display every passage from the new covenant (excluding the Gospels and Acts) that relates to the day of the catching away. The primary purpose of this chapter is to reveal how many references there are to the day of the catching away. As you will see, with so many references, the day of the catching away is very important in the agenda of God the Father. This chapter is also meant to be in commentary like format so you can take your time and do some valuable study on this topic.

The phrase *catching away* is the English equivalent to the Latin word *raptus,* better known as the *rapture.* This phrase derives from the passage in 1 Thessalonians chapter four, where it indicates that those who are abiding in the LORD (this is what it means to be in the LORD), whether they have already passed on physically or still alive physically, "will be caught up together with them in the clouds to meet the LORD in the air" (1 Thessalonians 4:17a, HNV). The Greek word Paul uses is *harpazo,* which suggests we will be *snatched up immediately by force* out of this physical realm. This concurs with what Paul wrote in 1 Corinthians 15:51–52: "We will all be changed, in a moment, in the twinkling of an eye." If we are to be changed in as fast as it takes an eye to blink, it must be one mighty powerful force that removes us out of this physical realm!

> For I consider that the sufferings of this present time are not worthy to be compared with the glory which will be revealed toward us, for the creation waits with eager expectation for the sons of God to be revealed. For the creation was subjected to vanity, not of its own will, but because of him who subjected it, in hope that the creation itself also will be delivered from the bondage of decay into the liberty of the glory of the children of God. For we know that the whole creation groans and travails in pain together until now. Not only so, but ourselves also, who have the first fruits of the Spirit, even we ourselves groan within ourselves, waiting for adoption, the redemption of our body; for we were saved in hope, but hope that is seen is not hope. For who hopes for that which he sees? But if we hope for that which we don't see, we wait for it with patience.

> Romans 8:18–25

- "The glory which will be revealed toward us." This phrase refers to the day when our earthly bodies will be changed into glorified spiritual bodies. Our new spiritual body will reflect the glory of the Father, just as Jesus's spiritual body does likewise.

- "The sons of God to be revealed." This is the same event when the sons and daughters of God will be completely redeemed, spirit, soul, and body.
- "The redemption of our body." This phrase represents salvation complete, which is eternal salvation.
- "We wait for it with patience." The sons and daughters of God have been waiting patiently for this day (or at least we are supposed to be) when our salvation is complete. We have been waiting ever since the first person who was abiding in Christ passed on.

Love doesn't harm a neighbor. Love therefore is the fulfillment of the law. Do this, knowing the time, that it is already time for you to awaken out of sleep, for salvation is now nearer to us than when we first believed.

Romans 13:10–11

- "For salvation is now nearer to us than when we first believed." This speaks of the salvation of our physical bodies, which is eternal salvation (see Hebrews 5:9; Romans 8:23; Philippians 3:21). Eternal salvation is when our physical body is changed into a spiritual body, which will never have an ending. Our physical body that has received salvation does come to end at some point, either through physical death or the catching away. But our spiritual body will never have an ending; this is what eternal salvation means. Paul had to be referring to eternal salvation in this passage, because his readers had already received initial salvation when they first believed. As each day goes by, the redemption of our bodies, which will make our salvation complete, gets closer. This becomes a reality on the day of the catching away.

> So that you come behind in no gift; waiting for the revelation of our LORD Yeshua [Jesus] the Messiah [Christ]; who will also confirm you until the end, blameless in the day of our LORD Yeshua [Jesus] the Messiah [Christ].
>
> 1 Corinthians 1:7–8

- "The revelation of the LORD Jesus Christ." The revelation of the LORD is the hour when the Christ comes for his people, which is the day he manifests himself to the church in his glorified spiritual body. We will then see the LORD Jesus Christ as he really is. (See 1 John 3:2.)
- "Confirm you until the end" refers to Christ being able to keep every faithful believer spiritually strong until the end of their physical life.
- "Blameless in the day of our LORD." The day of the LORD refers to the day of the catching away, in which we will be presented to him blameless, without sin.

> But if anyone builds on the foundation with gold, silver, costly stones, wood, hay, or stubble, each man's work will be revealed. For the day will declare it, because it is revealed in fire, and the fire itself will test what sort of work each man's work is. If any man's work remains which he built on it, he will receive a reward; if any man's work is burned, he will suffer loss, but he himself will be saved, but as through fire.
>
> 1 Corinthians 3:12–15

- "Builds on the foundation." This phrase represents the foundation of the household of God (the church), which the apostles and prophets began with Christ as the chief cornerstone (see Ephesians 2:19–22).

- "Each man's work will be revealed." Every believer will have their ministry to the church examined, or better said, put on trial. It will be proven whether we ministered with the material of heaven or the material of self.

- "For the day will declare it." The day that each man's work is revealed is the day of the catching away or just shortly after it. The day of the catching away is the genesis of this event.

- "He himself will be saved." This phrase sounds like a contradiction because Scripture says we are already saved. But this is not referring to initial salvation that we received when we first believed, but rather it refers to eternal salvation, when salvation is complete. Some will have their works destroyed because of the material they used (it is to their loss), but they will still partake in eternal salvation.

Therefore, judge nothing before the time, until the LORD comes, who will both bring to light the hidden things of darkness, and reveal the counsels of the hearts. Then each man will get his praise from God

1 Corinthians 4:5

- "Judge nothing before the time, until the LORD comes." This refers to the day of the catching away.

In the name of our Lord Yeshua [Jesus] the Messiah [Christ], you being gathered together, and my spirit, with the power of our Lord Yeshua [Jesus] the Messiah [Christ], are to deliver such a one to Hasatan [Satan] for the destruction of the flesh, that the spirit may be saved in the day of the Lord Yeshua [Jesus].

1 Corinthians 5:4–5

- "The spirit may be saved." Paul is speaking about this particular man's spirit being salvaged because he has corrupted it.
- "In the day of the Lord." The day of the Lord is the day of the catching away.

For as often as you eat this bread and drink this cup, you proclaim the Lord's death until he comes.

1 Corinthians 11:26

- "Until he comes" refers to the day of the catching away.

But now Messiah [Christ] has been raised from the dead. He became the first fruits of those who are asleep. For since death came by man, the resurrection of the dead also came by man; for as in Adam all die, so also in Messiah [Christ] all will be made alive. But each in his own order: Messiah [Christ] the first fruits, then those who are Messiah's [Christ's], at his coming.

1 Corinthians 15:20–23

- "Those who are asleep" represents those who have died physically and were abiding in Christ or rather remained in Jesus (the vine) until their death (see John 15:1–8).
- "In Messiah [Christ] all will be made alive." Make sure you see the intent of this statement, which is, all who were abiding in Christ when they died physically. They will be resurrected into glorified spiritual bodies forever.
- "At his coming"; this is the day of the catching away.

Now I say this, brothers, that flesh and blood can't inherit the kingdom of God; neither does corruption inherit incorruption. Behold, I tell you a mystery. We will not all sleep, but we will all be changed, in a moment, in the twinkling of an eye, at the last shofar [trumpet]. For the shofar [trumpet] will sound, and the dead will be raised incorruptible, and we will be changed. For this corruptible must put on incorruption, and this mortal must put on immortality. But when this corruptible will have put on incorruption, and this mortal will have put on immortality, then what is written will happen: "Death is swallowed up in victory."

1 Corinthians 15:50–54

- "I tell you a mystery." This is one of the mysteries of the kingdom of heaven that only those with ears to hear and eyes to see can understand.
- "We will not all sleep, but we will all be changed." On the day of the catching away there will be those who will be caught up while still alive in their physical body and will be changed from physical to spiritual.

- "The dead will be raised incorruptible, and we will be changed." Those who were in Christ and fallen asleep will receive an incorruptible body (glorified spiritual body).
- "The shofar [trumpet] will sound": The trumpet blast will sound at the catching away of those in Christ (see 1 Thessalonians 4:13–18).

For we write no other things to you, than what you read or even acknowledge, and I hope you will acknowledge to the end; as also you acknowledged us in part, that we are your boasting, even as you also are ours, in the day of our LORD Yeshua [Jesus].

2 Corinthians 1:13–14

- "In the day of our LORD Yeshua [Jesus]." This is another reference to the day of the catching away (have you been counting?). Paul and his associates will be able to boast in the day of the LORD that they conducted themselves amongst the Corinthian believers in a godly manner. Likewise, the Corinthian believers can boast that Paul and his associates did as said.

But having the same spirit of faith, according to that which is written, "I believed, and therefore I spoke." We also believe, and therefore also we speak; knowing that he who raised the LORD Yeshua [Jesus] will raise us also with Yeshua [Jesus], and will present us with you.

2 Corinthians 4:13–14

- "He who raised the Lᴏʀᴅ Yeshua [Jesus] will raise us also with Yeshua [Jesus]." God the Father, though the Holy Spirit, will resurrect the Apostles (and us) as he resurrected Jesus.

- "And will present us with you." The apostles, along with those in Christ, will be presented to the Father (implied) with Christ Jesus on the day of the catching away (see also Ephesians 5:27).

For we know that if the earthly house of our tent is dissolved, we have a building from God, a house not made with hands, eternal, in the heavens. For most assuredly in this we groan, longing to be clothed with our habitation which is from heaven; if so be that being clothed we will not be found naked. For indeed we who are in this tent do groan, being burdened; not that we desire to be unclothed, but that we desire to be clothed, that what is mortal may be swallowed up by life. Now he who made us for this very thing is God, who also gave to us the down payment of the Spirit. Being therefore always of good courage, and knowing that, while we are at home in the body, we are absent from the Lᴏʀᴅ; for we walk by faith, not by sight. We are of good courage, I say, and are willing rather to be absent from the body, and to be at home with the Lᴏʀᴅ.

2 Corinthians 5:1–8

- "The earthly house of our tent." This is symbolic of our physical body.
- "A house not made with hands." This is symbolic of our glorified spiritual body.

- "In this we groan, longing to be clothed with our habitation which is from heaven … We who are in this tent do groan, being burdened … But that we desire to be clothed." Our spirit longs to be clothed with our glorified spiritual body because "that what is mortal may be swallowed up by life." Our spirit is longing for its house made of the eternal life substance, which is a spiritual substance like Jesus has now, that allows him to be a man yet be made of a spiritual substance. We receive this only at the day of the catching away described in 1 Corinthians 15:50–54 and 1 Thessalonians 4:13–18.

- "Now he who made us for this very thing is God." This refers to God's will, which is that we be clothed with our habitation, which is from heaven. This heavenly habitation is only for those who were made new creations and held fast to the end to receive eternal salvation.

- "Gave to us the down payment of the Spirit." The Holy Spirit is proof that God willed that we be clothed with our habitation from heaven because Christ paid the price.

- "While we are at home in the body, we are absent from the LORD." "I say, and are willing rather to be absent from the body and to be at home with the LORD." While we are in our earthly habitation (body), we are away from the LORD (his literal physical presence). Until we receive our glorified spiritual body, we will not be completely with the LORD because right now we lack our spiritual house. Our spirit may be with him (referring to those who are asleep), but until our spirit receives our spiritual habitation, which will make us complete, we are not fully at home with the

Lord. Our life does not end once the catching away takes place; it actually just begins a new phase.

For we must all be revealed before the judgment seat of Messiah; that each one may receive the things in the body, according to what he has done, whether good or bad.

2 Corinthians 5:10

- "We must all be revealed before the judgment seat of Messiah." This refers to an event after we receive our glorified spiritual bodies.

In whom you also, having heard the word of the truth, the Good News of your salvation,—in whom, having also believed, you were sealed with the Ruach [Holy] HaKodesh [Spirit] of promise, who is a pledge of our inheritance, to the redemption of God's own possession, to the praise of his glory.

Ephesians 1:13–14

- "The redemption of God's own possession." This phrase is speaking about those who are God's possession (the new creation) having their salvation completed, which takes place the day of the catching away when we finally receive our glorified spiritual body. It is the salvation process being completely finished. It is the good work that God performed in those who have become partakers of Christ who are God's own possession, because each held fast their confidence in Christ from the beginning of their salvation, firm to the end of their redemption process (see Hebrews 3:6, 14)

Husbands, love your wives, even as Messiah [Christ] also loved the assembly [church], and gave himself up for it; that he might sanctify it, having cleansed it by the washing of water with the word, that he might present the assembly [church] to himself gloriously, not having spot or wrinkle or any such thing; but that it should be holy and without blemish.

Ephesians 5:25–27

- "That he might present the assembly [church] to himself gloriously." This is the day when the church body is finally completed (the end of the church age), which is the day of the catching away. The church will be glorious because the salvation process will be finished with our physical bodies along with our soul, finally being completely redeemed as our spirit was the very first day of our salvation. Our spirit, soul, and body will have no more imperfection. It will not even know how to sin anymore. This is Christ's wedding day, when he comes to receive his bride (see John 3:29; 14:1–4; 2 Corinthians 11:2). This is why we hold fast our confidence and the glorying of our hope firm to the end (see Hebrews 3:1, 6).

Being confident of this very thing that he who began a good work in you will complete it until the day of Yeshua [Jesus] the Messiah [Christ].

Philippians 1:6

- "He who began a good work in you will complete it until the day of Yeshua [Jesus]." God works his good work in every believer (if he is permitted by the one who has received salvation), which is the salvation process. He does this good work right up until the day of the catching away, which then culminates in our salvation being finally complete.

This I pray, that your love may abound yet more and more in knowledge and all discernment; so that you may approve the things that are excellent; that you may be sincere and without offense to the day of Messiah [Christ]; being filled with the fruits of righteousness, which are through Yeshua [Jesus] the Messiah [Christ], to the glory and praise of God.

Philippians 1:9–10

- "To the day of Messiah [Christ]." The day of Christ is the day of the catching away. The apostle Paul prays that the Philippians, which extends to the whole church, may abound in love to the day of Christ so knowledge and discernment will be able to reveal to us that salvation's work, which is living the righteous life, will bring glory to the Father. The love is in reference to God himself because he is love, working through us to one another.

Do all things without murmurings and disputes, that you may become blameless and harmless, children of God without blemish in the midst of a crooked and perverse generation, among whom you are seen as lights in the world, holding up the Word of life; that I may have something to boast in the day of Messiah [Christ], that I didn't run in vain nor labor in vain.

Philippians 2:14–16

- "That I may have something to boast in the day of Messiah [Christ]." This sentence refers to the day of the catching away. Paul knows that his labor will have not been in vain if those whom he taught, either in person or through his Holy Spirit-inspired writings, will have "become blameless and harmless, children of God without blemish in the midst of a crooked and perverse generation." Paul says he will have this to boast about, meaning his hard work, convincing those who received salvation to live like Christ so we can be without blemish. Becoming blameless and harmless children of God without blemish must be expected of us, or Paul would not say this is what we are to achieve.

Brothers, be imitators together of me, and note those who walk this way, even as you have us for an example. For many walk, of whom I told you often, and now tell you even weeping, as the enemies of the cross of Messiah [Christ], whose end is destruction, whose god is the belly, and whose glory is in their shame, who think about earthly things. For our citizenship is in heaven, from where we also wait for a Savior, the LORD Yeshua [Jesus] the Messiah [Christ]; who will change the body of our humiliation to be conformed to the body of his glory, according to the working by which he is able even to subject all things to himself.

Philippians 3:17–21

- "Who will change the body of our humiliation to be conformed to the body of his glory." On the day of the catching away, Christ will give us glorified spiritual bodies (see 1 Corinthians 15:50–54). The body of our humiliation speaks of our earthly habitation.

- "Our citizenship is in heaven, from where we also wait for a Savior, the LORD Yeshua [Jesus]." This suggests that we are consciously supposed to be waiting for the day of the catching away, because we are citizens of heaven (the eternal realm), where the Father is.

- "The enemies of the cross of Messiah [Christ]…" Take note of the description Paul gives of this group: They "think about earthly things," meaning they would always be focused on the pleasures of this world instead of the kingdom. They think highly of their fleshly desires, and they have made their stomach to be like a god, because they live to please it rather than living to please God. "Their end is destruction."

> If then you were raised together with Messiah [Christ], seek the things that are above, where Messiah [Christ] is, seated on the right hand of God. Set your mind on the things that are above, not on the things that are on the eretz [earth]; for you died, and your life is hidden with Messiah [Christ] in God. When Messiah [Christ], our life, is revealed, then you will also be revealed with him in glory.
>
> Colossians 3:1–4

- "When Messiah [Christ], our life, is revealed, then you will also be revealed with him in glory." We will be revealed with Christ Jesus on the day of the catching away.

- "If then you were raised together with Messiah [Christ]" refers to every Christian who was raised to newness of life in Christ because by faith received God's salvation (see Romans 6:1–4).

For from you has sounded forth the Word of the LORD, not only in Macedonia and Achaia, but also in every place your faith toward God has gone forth; so that we need not to say anything. For they themselves report concerning us what kind of a reception we had from you; and how you turned to God from idols, to serve a living and true God, and to wait for his Son from heaven, whom he raised from the dead— Yeshua [Jesus], who delivers us from the wrath to come.

1 Thessalonians 1:8–10

- "And to wait for his Son from heaven." This congregation was waiting for the Son to return, which has the meaning they were in a place of expectation. If they were in a place of expectation for the Son to return back then, then at what level of expectation should we be at especially with the revelation we have now?

- "Your faith toward God has gone forth … " "You turned to God from idols, to serve a living and true God … " Their faith in God included waiting for his Son to come and catch them away. In fact, this passage does suggest that as soon as the Thessalonians put their faith in God, their desire was to see Jesus come for them. Paul is actually commending them for this, not criticizing them as is the case in this generation.

- "Who delivers us from the wrath to come." We are *caught up* before the wrath to come, which takes place in the seventieth week of Israel (the Tribulation period).

For what is our hope, or joy, or crown of rejoicing? Isn't it even you, before our LORD Yeshua [Jesus] at his coming?

1 Thessalonians 2:19

- "Before our Lord Yeshua [Jesus] at his coming." Another reference to the day of the catching away.

> Now may our God and Father himself, and our Lord Yeshua [Jesus] the Messiah [Christ], direct our way to you; and the Lord make you to increase and abound in love one toward another, and toward all men, even as we also do toward you, to the end he may establish your hearts blameless in holiness before our God and Father, at the coming of our Lord Yeshua [Jesus] with all his holy ones.
>
> 1 Thessalonians 3:11–13

- "To the end he may establish your hearts blameless in holiness before our God and Father." "To the end" of our salvation process, the Lord's objective is to bring about our heart (spirit) without sin (blameless) in holiness (purity). Even though our spirit was made new (sin removed) at salvation, the Lord work's is to keep it that way. This is accomplished as the Lord makes us (if we are willing participants) to increase and abound in love one toward another and toward all men. When we became new creations, the salvation process was started, but the process must continue until the end of said process, which is the day of the redemption of our bodies. The purpose is for Jesus to present his holy ones (the pre-Tribulation saints, which is the church) to the Father without spot or wrinkle (holy without blemish) at the day of the catching away (see Ephesians 5:25–27).

- "At the coming of our Lord Yeshua [Jesus]." This refers to the day of the catching away.

- "With all his holy ones." This refers to the pre-Tribulation saints (the church), who are those us of who have received the redemption of our physical bodies, which is eternal salvation (on the day of the catching away). There will be millions of Tribulation saints, but they will not be resurrected until the first resurrection (see Revelation 20:4–6). It is important to understand that this passage does not refer to the "second coming," as some have thought, but rather it refers to the day of the catching away. A more appropriate way of interpreting this passage is this: Paul's desire is that when Jesus comes for the church, the Thessalonians' hearts be holy without blemish, along with the rest of the holy ones (saints).

But we don't want you to be ignorant, brothers, concerning those who have fallen asleep, so that you don't grieve like the rest, who have no hope. For if we believe that Yeshua [Jesus] died and rose again, even so those who have fallen asleep in Yeshua [Jesus] will God bring with him. For this we tell you by the Word of the LORD, that we who are alive, who are left to the coming of the LORD, will in no way precede those who have fallen asleep. For the LORD himself will descend from heaven with a shout, with the voice of the chief angel, and with God's shofar [trumpet]. The dead in Messiah [Christ] will rise first, then we who are alive, who are left, will be caught up together with them in the clouds, to meet the LORD in the air. So we will be with the LORD forever. Therefore comfort one another with these words.

1 Thessalonians 4:13–18

- This passage is a description of *the hour* of the catching away of the church. It parallels with 1 Corinthians 15:51–54 and also with the parable of the ten virgins, in particular, Matthew 25:6, 10, and 13.

- "God bring with him." This reveals that it is the Father who *snatches us up* to meet Jesus.

- "So those who have fallen asleep in Yeshua [Jesus]..." "The dead in Messiah [Christ]...": This refers to those who have already died physically and who were abiding in Jesus (In Jesus: see John 15:4–6).

- It was for this day that the Father carried on his good work in us (see Philippians 1:6) pruning us so we bear (more) and much fruit so his name is glorified (see John 15:2, 8).

But concerning the times and the seasons, brothers, you have no need that anything be written to you. For you yourselves know well that the day of the LORD comes like a thief in the night. For when they are saying, "Shalom [Peace] and safety," then sudden destruction will come on them, like birth pains on a pregnant woman; and they will in no way escape. But you, brothers, aren't in darkness, that the day should overtake you like a thief. You are all sons of light, and sons of the day. We don't belong to the night, nor to darkness, so then let's not sleep, as the rest do, but let's watch and be sober. For those who sleep, sleep in the night, and those who are drunken are drunken in the night. But let us, since we belong to the day, be sober, putting on the breastplate of faith and love, and, for a helmet, the hope of salvation. For God didn't appoint us to wrath, but to the obtaining of salvation through our LORD Yeshua [Jesus] the Messiah [Christ], who died for us, that, whether we wake or sleep, we should live together with him. Therefore exhort one another, and build each other up, even as you also do.

1 Thessalonians 5:1–11

- "For you yourselves know well that the day of the Lord comes like a thief in the night ... But you, brothers, aren't in darkness, that the day should overtake you like a thief": These verses refer to those of us who are the redeemed of the Lord, having knowledge of the day of the catching away because we are not in darkness. We have knowledge because we study the Word. Therefore, God reveals to us the approximate time of the second coming and the catching away prior to that. That is why Paul said to the Thessalonians and to us that there was no need for him to write about the time and the season of the day of the Lord because we are sons of the light, meaning we live in the light and have insight into the Word. We already have the knowledge of the time and season if we listen to the Word of God (study Matthew chapter 24, Mark chapter 13, and Luke chapter 21). The day of the Lord comes like a "thief in the night" only to those who are in the darkness not to those who are of the light.

- "For when they are saying, 'Shalom [Peace] and safety,' then sudden destruction will come on them, like birth pains on a pregnant woman; and they will in no way escape." This refers to the hour of the catching away, when most of those in darkness will not be expecting the sudden change upon the earth once hundreds of millions of people suddenly disappear from the earth. Up to this point, those in darkness are living in considerable peace and safety around the world. It does not mean the whole earth will be at peace, because the world is never completely safe from the evils of the world until Jesus sets up his millennial kingdom. But once the redeemed of the Lord are caught up to meet him in the air there will be utter chaos on the earth. This will make their troubles at that point pale in comparison. It will all happen as fast as the first contraction pains a woman experiences when she is ready to give birth.

- "We don't belong to the night, nor to darkness, so then let's not sleep, as the rest do, but let's watch and be sober." This is parallel with the parable of the ten virgins (see Matthew 25:2–5, 13).

- "But let us, since we belong to the day, be sober, putting on the breastplate of faith and love and for a helmet, the hope of salvation." In this verse pay particular attention to the phrase "the hope of salvation," which refers to salvation complete, the redemption of the body. We put our hope in the Lord for this day, being fitted with faith and love.

- "For God didn't appoint us to wrath." The appointment of wrath refers to the Tribulation period (Israel's seventieth-week period; see Daniel 9:27 and Revelation 6–19).

- "But to the obtaining of salvation through our Lord Yeshua [Jesus] the Messiah [Christ]..." This refers to obtaining *salvation complete* through the author of eternal salvation (see Hebrews 5:9 and 2 Timothy 2:10).

May the God of shalom [peace] himself sanctify you completely. May your whole spirit, soul, and body be preserved blameless at the coming of our Lord Yeshua [Jesus] the Messiah [Christ]. Faithful is he who calls you, who will also do it.

1 Thessalonians 5:23–24

- "May the God of shalom [peace] himself sanctify you completely." This sentence indicates that it is God's desire to make our soul and body holy just as our spirit was made holy when we first received salvation. When we first put our faith in Jesus, our spirit was made holy, thus we became new creations. Now God does his good work in us to make us completely holy or sanctified. Paul says "May God," which has the meaning "God will do it, if we let him" (we have to literally give him permission).

- "May your whole spirit, soul, and body be preserved blameless." This is speaking of our complete being, meaning our spirit, soul, and body, maintaining the sanctifying work of God, which is holiness in all three parts. Again Paul says "May your," which implies we must be a willing participant.

- "At the coming of our LORD Yeshua [Jesus] the Messiah [Christ]." The coming of the LORD refers to the day of the catching away of the church.

- "Faithful is he who calls you, who will also do it." God the Father is faithful to do his part, because this is what he called us to.

Since it is a righteous thing with God to repay affliction to those who afflict you and to give relief to you that are afflicted with us, when the LORD Yeshua [Jesus] is revealed from heaven with his mighty angels in flaming fire, giving vengeance to those who don't know God, and to those who don't obey the Good News of our LORD Yeshua [Jesus], who will pay the penalty: eternal destruction from the face of the LORD and from the glory of his might, when he comes to be glorified in his holy ones, and to be admired among all those who have believed (because our testimony to you was believed) in that day.

2 Thessalonians 1:6–10

- This passage refers to the second coming and not the catching away. Paul is reassuring all those who have suffered persecutions and afflictions because of Christ and the gospel that God will repay those who have caused this upon his holy ones at the second coming.

Now, brothers, concerning the coming of our LORD Yeshua [Jesus] the Messiah [Christ], and our gathering together to him, we ask you not to be quickly shaken in your mind, nor yet be troubled, either by spirit, or by word, or by letter as from us, saying that the day of Messiah [Christ] had come. Let no one deceive you in any way. For it will not be, unless the departure comes first, and the man of sin is revealed, the son of destruction, he who opposes and exalts himself against all that is called God or that is worshiped; so that he sits as God in the temple of God, setting himself up as God. Don't you remember that, when I was still with you, I told you these things? Now you know what is restraining him, to the end that he may be revealed in his own season. For the mystery of lawlessness already works. Only there is one who restrains now, until he is taken out of the way. Then the lawless one will be revealed, whom the LORD will kill with the breath of his mouth, and bring to nothing by the brightness of his coming; even he whose coming is according to the working of Hasatan [Satan] with all power and signs and lying wonders, and with all deception of wickedness for those who are being lost, because they didn't receive the love of the truth, that they might be saved.

2 Thessalonians 2:1–10

- "The coming of our LORD Yeshua [Jesus]…Our gathering together to him…The day of Messiah [Christ]." These all refer to the day of the catching away.

- "The departure comes first." This statement reveals there will be a falling away from the faith. It literally means to forsake Christ. It is an apostasy from the Word of God through disobedience (see 1Timothy 4:1). The catching away of the church will happen after there is a falling away from faith in the LORD Jesus Christ and the Word of God. This is not referring to an odd occurrence, but it refers to an enormous number who depart from the faith within a short period of time.

- "The man of sin is revealed." The way Paul structures this statement confuses people about when the catching away takes place. Is it not until after the man of sin is revealed, as it seems to say in our English Bibles? If this is what Paul meant, then it would contradict Scripture, because the church age is suppose to end before the man of sin is revealed. The man of sin is the antichrist, who confirms a covenant with Israel, which begins Israel's seventieth week (see Daniel 9:27). The church age ends before Israel's seventieth week can begin (see Revelation). We see in this passage, starting at 2:6 to 2:8, that the man of sin will not be revealed until after the one who restrains "the mystery of lawlessness" is removed. That person who restrains "the mystery of lawlessness" is the church, who has been given the authority of Christ to do so. Christ gave us the authority and power of his Holy Spirit over the powers of darkness here on this earth, so during the church age the powers of the enemy have been limited because at

least some of the church has practiced Christ's authority, which restrains the powers of darkness (see Matthew
18:18; Mark 16:17–18; Luke 10:19; John 14:12; 2 Corinthians 10:4–5; Ephesians 2:6; 3:20–21). But once we are
removed through the catching away, the powers of darkness will have the freedom to deceive men like they had
before Christ was raised from the dead and the church age
began. Thus, the "man of sin" goes headstrong deceiving
Israel and most Gentiles and makes a covenant with Israel,
which begins Israel's seventieth-week period where Israel
is deceived into believing the "man of sin" is their Messiah. What is concluded is, that we through translational
error, have worded the original Greek out of order, but
even more likely it is just a matter of punctuation blunder.
We must keep in mind that the original documents and
the earliest manuscripts contained no punctuation. In fact,
the Scriptures were written in "continuous script," which
means there were no spaces between words or sentences,
along with the absence of punctuation. Punctuation was
not inserted into the Bible until at least the fifth century
(some believe even later than that), so there is the possibility, as in this case, that a comma misplaced can contradict
the original intent of the writer. As said, verses six to eight
show that the man of sin is revealed after the church is
taken up. So to keep this phrase "the departure comes first,
and the man of sin is revealed" from contradicting verses
six to eight, as it seems to in so many English translations,
the punctuation mark quite possibly should be a period
instead of a comma between the word *first* and the word
and. This would give the phrase a clear break in the writers

intentional thought thus keeping verses six to eight from sounding like a contradiction.

- "And bring to nothing by the brightness of his coming." This verse pertains to the second coming and not the catching away, when Christ comes with his church at the end of the Tribulation period to redeem Israel.

I charge you before God, who gives life to all things, and before Messiah [Christ] Yeshua [Jesus], who before Pontius Pilate testified the good confession, that you keep the mitzvah [commandment] without spot, blameless, until the appearing of our LORD Yeshua [Jesus] the Messiah [Christ]; which in its own times he will show, who is the blessed and only Ruler, the King of kings, and LORD of LORDS.

1 Timothy 6:13–15

- "Until the appearing of our LORD Yeshua [Jesus] the Messiah [Christ]." This refers to the day of the catching away.

For this cause I suffer also these things. Yet I am not ashamed, for I know him whom I have believed, and I am persuaded that he is able to guard that which I have committed to him against that day.

2 Timothy 1:12

- "He is able to guard that which I have committed to him against that day." This is saying that God is able to keep us, as we are committed to him right up to the day of the catching away.

May the Lord grant mercy to the house of Onesiphorus, for he often refreshed me, and was not ashamed of my chain, but when he was in Rome, he sought me diligently, and found me (the Lord grant to him to find the Lord's mercy in that day); and in how many things he served at Ephesus, you know very well.

2 Timothy 1:16–18

- "The Lord grant to him to find the Lord's mercy in that day." Paul is referring to the day of the catching away.

I charge you therefore before God and the Lord Yeshua [Jesus] the Messiah [Christ], who will judge the living and the dead at his appearing and his kingdom.

2 Timothy 4:1

- "Who will judge the living and the dead at his appearing and his kingdom." This is referring to the catching away, even though it sounds like the second coming. Keeping within the context of Paul's instruction to Timothy, Paul is speaking about ministers preaching the Word according to God's will and not the will of the people (see verses 2–5). When Christ comes for his church, there will be a time of judgment for his people, as it says in 2 Corinthians 2:10: "For we must all be revealed (manifest to) before the judgment seat of Messiah; that each one may receive the things in the body, according to what he has done, whether good or bad." The people whom Paul is referring to in this passage "the living and the dead" are in reference to "those who are alive" and "those who have fallen asleep" (1 Thessalonians 4:15) at the day of the catching away.

For I am already being offered, and the time of my departure has come. I have fought the good fight. I have finished the course. I have kept the faith. From now on, there is stored up for me the crown of righteousness, which the LORD, the righteous judge, will give to me on that day; and not to me only, but also to all those who have loved his appearing.

2 Timothy 4:6–8

- "His appearing" and "will give to me on that day" refer to the day of the catching away.
- "I have kept the faith." This is Paul holding fast his confession in Christ until the end of his physical life (see Hebrews 4:14; 10:23).
- "There is stored up for me the crown of righteousness...Those who have loved his appearing..." Paul speaks about a *special crown* that will be presented to those who have had a deep longing for day of the catching away.

For the grace of God has appeared, bringing salvation to all men, instructing us to the intent that, denying ungodliness and worldly lusts, we would live soberly, righteously, and godly in this present world; looking for the blessed hope and appearing of the glory of our great God and Savior, Yeshua [Jesus] the Messiah [Christ]; who gave himself for us, that he might redeem us from all iniquity, and purify for himself a people for his own possession, zealous for good works. Say these things.

Titus 2:11–15a

- "The blessed hope and appearing of the glory of our great God and Savior." This refers to the day of the catching away, when we will see his glory (him in his glorified spiritual body).

- "Looking for the blessed hope and appearing..." Paul reveals that we are to be *looking for* the day of the catching away rather than being indifferent about it.

- "The grace of God has appeared, bringing salvation to all men." But all men have to receive God's grace and then abide in his grace.

- "Denying ungodliness and worldly lusts, we would live soberly, righteously, and godly in this present world." The Word of God teaches us how to live in accordance with the grace of God.

- "Say these things..." This indicates that denying ungodliness and worldly lusts, living in the righteousness of God, and looking for the day of the catching away are to be taught.

> So Messiah also, having been once offered to bear the sins of many, will appear a second time, without sin, to those who are eagerly waiting for him for salvation.
>
> Hebrews 9:28

- "Will appear a second time." This refers to the day of the catching away and not the second coming. Some have been confused with this because of the phrase *second time*, thereby thinking this means the second coming. The context of this passage is that Christ came once to bear the sins of many, and then he comes a second time to gather up those who are "waiting for him." The phrase *second coming* is actually a misnomer, because Jesus actually comes three times to his people. He came the first time to present himself as Israel's king. He comes the second time to gather up the church. He comes the third time to redeem Israel. So he actually comes to his people *three times*. The reason we use the term *second coming* is to indicate that Jesus comes to literally set his feet on the earth again, as he did at his first coming. When he comes for the church his feet do not touch the earth, so this is why we use the phrase *second coming* to describe the difference between the two events (the rapture and to redeem Israel). Scripture never does refer to Jesus coming at the end of Israel's seventieth week as his second coming. It is the church who has attached this phrase to this powerful event.

- "To those who are eagerly waiting for him for salvation." This refers to eternal salvation when our bodies will finally be redeemed. Take special notice that the Christ appears a *second time* to bring salvation (to the body and the soul) of those who are eagerly waiting for him!

> Let us consider how to provoke one another to love and good works, not forsaking our own assembling together, as the custom of some is, but exhorting one another; and so much the more, as you see the day approaching.
>
> Hebrews 10:24–25

- "As you see the day approaching..." This refers to the day of the catching away. To see the *day* approaching, we need to be watching for it (see Matthew 24:42, 44; 25:13).

Be patient therefore, brothers, until the coming of the
LORD. Behold, the farmer waits for the precious fruit of the
eretz [earth], being patient over it, until it receives the early
and late rain. You also be patient. Establish your hearts, for
the coming of the LORD is at hand.

James 5:7–8

- "The coming of the LORD ... The coming of the LORD is at hand ..." These are references to the day of the catching away.

- "Be patient therefore, brothers." We must be patient for the coming of the LORD, because it will come at the time of the appointed season. (There is an appointed Day; see Matthew 24:36; Mark 13:32.)

- "Establish your hearts." This is an indication that we are to make our spirit strong by standing fast in the Word and our faith in Christ.

Blessed be the God and Father of our LORD Yeshua [Jesus]
the Messiah [Christ], who according to his great mercy
became our father again to a living hope through the resurrection of Yeshua [Jesus] the Messiah [Christ] from the
dead, to an incorruptible and undefiled inheritance that
doesn't fade away, reserved in heaven for you, who by the
power of God are guarded through faith for a salvation
ready to be revealed in the last time.

1 Peter 1:3–5

- "An incorruptible and undefiled inheritance that doesn't fade away ..." The inheritance being referred to here is the glori-fied spiritual body we receive (like Christ has now) on the day of the catching away (see 1 Corinthians 9:24–27; 15:51–54).

- "Reserved in heaven for you..." We will receive it once our salvation is complete.

- "A salvation ready to be revealed in the last time..." The salvation being referred to is eternal salvation, which is our salvation complete, body, soul, and spirit. It will be revealed to us in the last time of the church, meaning the time when the church is completed. This will commence on the day of the catching away.

- "Who by the power of God are guarded through faith..." This reveals that God's power will guard us until the last time of the church, as we keep our faith in the LORD Jesus Christ (see Hebrews 3:6, 14; 10:35–39).

> Wherein you greatly rejoice, though now for a little while, if need be, you have been put to grief in various trials, that the proof of your faith, which is more precious than gold that perishes even though it is tested by fire, may be found to result in praise, glory, and honor at the revelation of Yeshua [Jesus] the Messiah [Christ].
>
> 1 Peter 1:6–7

- "At the revelation of Yeshua [Jesus]." The revelation of Jesus is the appearing of the LORD at the day of the catching away.

- "The proof of your faith... may be found to result in praise, glory, and honor." Our faith in Christ must remain firm until that day.

> Whom not having known you love; in whom, though now you don't see him, yet believing, you rejoice greatly with joy

unspeakable and full of glory—receiving the result of your faith, the salvation of your souls

1 Peter 1:8–9

- "The salvation of your souls." This refers our mind, will, and emotions being made complete and fit for the presence of God the Father. Our spirit received salvation (made complete) the moment we put our faith in Christ—hence the term *new creation*—but our soul and body were left undone. Paul's writings show us that we must then cooperate with God as he works his salvation in us by renewing our mind (one part of the soul) (see Romans 12:2; and Philippians 2:12). We must likewise offer our body as a living sacrifice making it holy and acceptable to God, so he can transform us; body and soul (see Romans 12:1), taking our corruptible being and changing it into an incorruptible being, or in other words, transforming our earthly bodies into heavenly bodies (at his coming). We receive the salvation of our souls and body, which then makes salvation complete in our complete being of our person (spirit, soul and body) at the day of the catching away.

- "Receiving the result of your faith …" Again, this all comes to pass as a result of our faith being firm in Christ, holding on to our confession of him (see Hebrews 4:14; 10:23) to the end of our time in our earthly body.

Therefore, prepare your minds for action, be sober and set your hope fully on the grace that will be brought to you at the revelation of Yeshua [Jesus] the Messiah [Christ].

1 Peter 1:13

- "At the revelation of Yeshua [Jesus]..." The revelation of Jesus takes place the day the Lord appears at the catching away.

I exhort the Zakenim [Elders] among you, as a fellow elder, and a witness of the sufferings of Messiah [Christ], and who will also share in the glory that will be revealed. Shepherd the flock of God which is among you, exercising the oversight, not under compulsion, but voluntarily, not for dishonest gain, but willingly; neither as Lording it over the charge allotted to you, but making yourselves examples to the flock. When the chief Shepherd is revealed, you will receive the crown of glory that doesn't fade away.

1 Peter 5:1–4

- "Will also share in the glory that will be revealed..." The glory refers to the magnificence of Christ that will be revealed at the day of the catching away. The elders of the church will share in this glory with the rest of the body of Christ. For example, on this day we become like Christ, as it is written: "But we know that, when he is revealed, we will be like him; for we will see him just as he is" (1 John 3:2b).
- "When the chief Shepherd is revealed..." The Lord Jesus will be revealed (in his glory) on the day of the catching away.
- "The crown of glory that doesn't fade away..." Overseers of God's people will receive a crown of glory when the "chief Shepherd" is revealed; that will illuminate the splendor and magnificence of the Lord Jesus Christ, which will be brilliant forever.

This is now, beloved, the second letter that I have written to you; and in both of them I stir up your sincere mind by reminding you; that you should remember the words which were spoken before by the holy Prophets, and the mitzvoth [commandment] of us, the apostles of the LORD and Savior: knowing this first, that in the last days mockers will come, walking after their own lusts, and saying, "Where is the promise of his coming? For, from the day that the fathers fell asleep, all things continue as they were from the beginning of the creation.

2 Peter 3:1–4

- "In the last days." This refers to the last days of the church age, prior to Israel's seventieth week period.

- "Where is the promise of his coming?" The promise in question is the promise the LORD made to his disciples (and we by extension): "Don't let your heart be troubled. Believe in God. Believe also in me. In my Father's house are many mansions. If it weren't so, I would have told you. I am going to prepare a place for you. If I go and prepare a place for you, I will come again, and will receive you to myself; that where I am, you may be there also" (John 14:1–3). This day, that the LORD said he will come again refers to the day of the Catching away. It is this day that the mockers are treating with contempt because they walk after their own lusts, meaning they have their own agenda instead of submitting to the plans of the LORD. Who are these mockers treating this day with contempt? It is not those who are outside of the church culture, because these people have no depth of knowledge of the catching away. It must be people who are within the church culture who have been taught of the coming of the LORD in the same generation of the last days of the church age and are not fully convinced of the prophecies pertaining to the season. Let me ask everyone this question: How many have known someone who has spoken these words of disappointment to you, saying, "People who long for the LORD's coming are only trying to escape this world"? Or have you heard people within the church who have ridiculed those who even bring up the subject of the LORD's coming? Their ridicule may include "No one knows when the LORD will come, so we should not even entertain the thought." These people are whom Peter is referring to as mockers. Inwardly these people laugh at those who long for the LORD to come.

- "From the day that the fathers fell asleep, all things continue as they were from the beginning of the creation ..." This statement is the logic the mockers use to say, "Nothing changes. Every day is like the day before, so where is the LORD? Did he break his promise?" So now Peter turns their own words back on them in 2 Peter 3:5–7 by using the example of creation (using their own words) by saying that by God's own Word, creation exists, and by God's same Word, ungodly men who mock the Word of the LORD will be judged and destroyed. Peter states this to emphasize that by God's own Word, the LORD's coming in the last days is a reality.

But don't forget this one thing, beloved, that one day is with the LORD as a thousand years, and a thousand years as one day. The LORD is not slow concerning his promise, as some count slowness; but is patient with us, not wishing that any should perish, but that all should come to repentance.

2 Peter 3:8–9

- "His promise." This promise is the same promise in John 14:1–3, which is the day Christ comes for his church.

- "One day is with the LORD as a thousand years, and a thousand years as one day." With this statement, Peter is explaining that the LORD is not slow in keeping his promise. In the last days of the church age, it will be almost two thousand years since Christ made this promise to come for the church. So naturally, some will think the LORD is slow in keeping his promise, even to the point of doubting his promise, like the mockers. But using the analogy "One day is with the LORD as a thousand years, and a thousand years as one day," it has only been like two days to the LORD since he made this promise. Some have said this refers to the second coming, but we must remember, Peter is addressing the new creation here and not Israel. The second coming is the event when Jesus comes to save Israel, whereas the catching away is to complete the salvation process of the church of the Anointed One. The church is interested foremost in the day of the catching away so we can be fully redeemed. Of course we are also very interested in the second coming so Israel can receive her inheritance, but at that event, we will be coming with Jesus to be a part of this prophecy (see Jude 1:14).

But the day of the LORD will come as a thief in the night; in which the heavens will pass away with a great noise, and the elements will be dissolved with fervent heat, and the eretz [earth] and the works that are in it will be burned up.

2 Peter 3:10

- "But the day of the LORD will come as a thief in the night." This phrase refers to the day of the catching away. This statement is the same one Paul makes in 1 Thessalonians 5:2, but it also adds, "But you, brothers, aren't in darkness, that the day should overtake you like a thief" (1 Thessalonians 5:4). To those who are not ready for the catching away of the church it will come like a thief in the night because *that day and hour* will come so quickly to those who are not prepared. The rest of 2 Peter 3:10, along with 2 Peter 3:12, according to this translation of use and some others, seems to imply that once the day of the LORD occurs, creation will cease to exist immediately in its present form; but that is not the intention of this passage. The proper intent of this passage is that the present creation will change at some point in the future plan of God, but it cannot happen until after the day of the catching away comes first. We read in Romans 8:19–21 that creation waits with great patience for the church to be fully redeemed so it can be delivered from bondage of decay. Creation actually "groans and travails in pain" (Romans 8:22) because of what it has been subjected to. So once we receive our glorified spiritual bodies, creation will breathe a sigh of relief, knowing that its bondage to decay is soon over. As said, the earth and the heavens (not meaning heaven itself) in its present form will not pass away until way into the future, after we Christians are *caught up* to meet the LORD in the air. We read this in Revelation: "I saw a new heaven and a new eretz [earth]: for the first heaven and the first eretz [earth] have passed away, and the sea is no more" (Revelation 21:1). This event does not occur until after the 1,000-year reign of the LORD Jesus Christ on the earth, which is a great number of years after the catching away.

Now, little children, remain in him, that when he appears, we may have boldness, and not be ashamed before him at his coming.

1 John 2:28

- "When he appears … At his coming …" These two phrases refer to the day of the catching away.

Beloved, now we are children of God, and it is not yet revealed what we will be. But we know that, when he is revealed, we will be like him; for we will see him just as he is. Everyone who has this hope set on him purifies himself, even as he is pure.

1 John 3:2–3

- "When he is revealed …" This refers to the day of the catching away.
- "Everyone who has this hope set on him purifies himself." Everyone who has their hope set on Christ being revealed on the day of the catching away has a mindset of living a pure life. This mindset is something we must achieve because it has a purifying effect.

A pure life consists of living in the grace of God.

Bringing every thought into captivity to the obedience of Messiah.

2 Corinthians 10:5

What shall we say then? Shall we continue in sin, that grace may abound? May it never be! We who died to sin, how could we live in it any longer?

Romans 6:1–2

What then? Shall we sin, because we are not under law, but under grace? May it never be!

Romans 6:15

Thus also consider yourselves also to be dead to sin, but alive to God in Messiah [Christ] Yeshua [Jesus] our LORD.

Romans 6:11

He died for all, that those who live should no longer live to themselves, but to him who for their sakes died and rose again.

2 Corinthians 5:15

Forasmuch then as Messiah [Christ] suffered for us in the flesh, arm yourselves also with the same mind; for he who has suffered in the flesh has ceased from sin; that you no longer should live the rest of your time in the flesh for the lusts of men, but for the will of God. For we have spent enough of our past time living in doing the desire of the Goyim [Gentiles], and to have walked in lewdness, lusts, drunken binges, orgies, carousings, and abominable idolatries.

1 Peter 4:1–3

The whole of 1 John 3 suggests we who have received salvation have a responsibility to live in Christ like purity.

Behold, he is coming with the clouds, and every eye will see him, including those who pierced him. All the tribes of the eretz [earth] will mourn over him. Even so, Amein [Amen].

Revelation 1:7

- "He is coming with the clouds ..." This is *not* a reference to the *catching away* of the church, but it refers to the *second coming*. When Christ comes for the church, "every eye" will not see him, only those who are "caught up together with them in the clouds, to meet the LORD in the air" (1 Thessalonians 4:17). However, "every eye will see him" at the second coming "including those who pierced him."

But I have this against you, that you left your first love. Remember therefore from where you have fallen, and repent and do the first works; or else I am coming to you swiftly, and will move your menorah [lampstand] out of its place, unless you repent.

Revelation 2:4–5

- "I am coming to you swiftly." This is in reference to Jesus coming to get his church. Jesus does not come to the church until the day of the catching away; but when he comes, he will be coming swiftly to catch us up "in the twinkling of an eye" (1 Corinthians 15:52), which is pretty swift, I might add. Jesus is speaking to the portion of the church (represented by this Ephesians congregation) who has "left their first love," who is Jesus. "Left their first love" is cognitive to their relationship with Jesus, which has taken a step backward to their works. The church's first love is Jesus Christ, and it extends to the practice of obeying his commands to love one another. This particular Ephesians congregation was *working hard doing the right things*, except their love for Christ had diminished. To reiterate, this Ephesians congregation represents those in the church as a whole, through all generations, until the day of the catching away. There will be those in the church, even in this present generation, whom Jesus is speaking to right now, who have all the *right performances* but have left their first love. The Spirit says this, "If a man says, 'I love God,' and hates his brother, he is a liar; for he who doesn't love his brother whom he has seen, how can he love God whom he has not seen? This mitzvah [command] we have from him, that he who loves God should also love his brother" (1 John 4:20–21).

- "Will move your menorah [lamp-stand] out of its place, unless you repent": This is to be understood as literally, this lamp-stand being removed from within its position in Christ. The lamp-stand is the church (see Revelation 1:20). This lampstand has fallen and *unless it repents* of leaving its first love, will be removed because the Word of the LORD says: 1 John 4:8, "He who doesn't love doesn't know God, for God is love." When a person leaves their first love (Jesus and his commands), they are in the process of falling from grace. They must repent quickly because the LORD comes swiftly! As a reminder: "You don't know in what hour your LORD comes" (Matthew 24:42).

So you also have some who hold to the teaching of the Nicolaitans likewise. Repent therefore, or else I am coming to you quickly, and I will make war against them with the sword of my mouth.

Revelation 2:15–16

- "I am coming to you quickly." As said in the commentary for Revelation 2:5, Jesus comes for the church at *an hour that we do not know* and at the speed of how fast it takes the eye to blink. Jesus does not come for us until the day of the catching away and no sooner.

- "I will make war against them with the sword of my mouth." This has the connotation that the Word of God will stand to judge those who hold to this teaching of the Nicolations. The Nicolations doctrine was similar to the teaching of Balaam, which was that it was okay to eat food that was sacrificed to idols and commit sexual immorality. These things are, in actuality, prohibited for the church of Jesus Christ to partake in (see Acts 15:29; 21:25; and 1 Corinthians 8:4–8; 10:18–22). The apostle Peter said there will be those in the church who partake in this evil practice: "Who have forsaken the right way, and gone astray, following the way of Balaam [the son] of Bosor [Beor], who loved the wages of unrighteousness" (2 Peter 2:15).

But to you I say, to the rest who are in Thyatira, as many as don't have this teaching, who don't know what some call 'the deep things of Hasatan [Satan],' to you I say, I am not putting any other burden on you. Nevertheless, hold firmly that which you have, until I come.

Revelation 2:24–25

- "Until I come." This congregation was to "hold on firmly" to their devotion to God. That is, they do not participate in the teaching of the so-called prophetess, Jezebel, who was teaching the believers that it was okay "to commit sexual immorality and eat things sacrificed to animals." This passage implies that this group (and those who come after them) "must hold on firmly" to the Word of God until Jesus comes.

> Remember therefore how you have received and heard. Keep it, and repent. If therefore you won't watch, I will come as a thief, and you won't know what hour I will come upon you.
>
> Revelation 3:3

- "You won't know what hour I will come upon you." "The hour" refers to the moment when the trumpet will sound. This group (along with groups in this generation) will not know the hour of the catching away if they do not keep the Word of God and repent, which they have "received and heard." Jesus uses this same analogy of the thief in Matthew 24:42–44. Concerning the catching away, the church is not supposed to be caught off guard as those who do not know the LORD (see 1 Thessalonians 5:1–5).

> Because you kept my command to endure, I also will keep you from the hour of testing, which is to come on the whole world, to test those who dwell on the eretz [earth].
>
> Revelation 3:10

- "I also will keep you from the hour of testing." This implies that those who are "caught up to meet the LORD in the air" (1 Thessalonians 4:17) will be *caught up* before the Tribulation period (Israel's seventieth week) begins. But pay particular attention to the condition of being kept from the hour of testing, which is "because you kept my command to endure" and also, "kept my Word, and didn't deny my name" (Revelation 3:8).

I am coming quickly! Hold firmly that which you have, so that no one takes your crown.

Revelation 3:11

- "I am coming quickly." Jesus coming to catch the church up is fast approaching and will be "in the twinkling of an eye" (1 Corinthians 15:52). The church is to hang on to faith in Jesus Christ, so no one robs us (meaning the enemy) of our crown (likely the crown of eternal life).

After these things I looked and saw a door opened in heaven, and the first voice that I heard, like a shofar [trumpet] speaking with me, was one saying, "Come up here, and I will show you the things which must happen after this." Immediately I was in the Spirit. Behold, there was a throne set in heaven, and one sitting on the throne.

Revelation 4:1–2

- "Come up here…": These are the words we will hear immediately before we are snatched away into heaven. This passage is the rapture being revealed to the apostle John while he was in the Spirit. What follows in Revelation chapters four and five is what we will see, or be a part of, in heaven just after we are taken up into heaven (you will be blessed if you read it).

> Behold, I come quickly. Blessed is he who keeps the words of the prophecy of this book.
>
> Revelation 22:7

- "Behold, I come quickly." Another reference to the day of the catching away and that it is coming quickly.

> Behold, I come quickly. My reward is with me, to repay to each man according to his work.
>
> Revelation 22:12

- "Behold, I come quickly." Have you been counting how many references there are to the day of the catching away?

> He who testifies these things says, "Yes, I come quickly." Amein [Amen]! Yes, come, Lord Yeshua [Jesus].
>
> Revelation 22:20

- "Yes, I come quickly." This is one last reference to the day of the catching away.
- "Amein [Amen]! Yes, come, Lord Yeshua [Jesus]." Now the apostle John, after hearing the Lord Jesus Christ say he is coming quickly, agrees with him and says, "Yes come." This final generation of the church of the Lord should also be in agreement. Do you agree?

This book of the Revelation was written for those who are new creations (Jews and Gentiles made into a new man reconciled to God through faith in Jesus Christ. See Ephesians 2:14–18) to reveal God's future plan to us after we have been caught up. The implications of this phrase "I come quickly" spoken three times (in Revelations 22:7, 12, and 20) is to encourage every believer that "Yes, I [Jesus] come quickly" (Revelation 22:20a).

Peace to you!

Endnotes

1 "Ethiopic text of the Apocalypse of Peter": Traditional Version; Translation and Notes by M. R. James–1924; <http://mb-soft.com/believe/txh/peter2.htm>

2 "The Coming Prince" by Sir Robert Anderson: Philologos Religious Online Books; November 12, 2009 < http://philologos.org/__eb-tcp/default.htm>

3 "The Coming Prince" by Sir Robert Anderson: Philologos Religious Online Books; November 12, 2009 < http://philologos.org/__eb-tcp/default.htm>

4 "Armageddon, Appointment with Destiny" by Dr. Grant Jeffrey; Published by WaterBrook Press (Originally published by Frontier Research Publications): 1997

5 "Armageddon, Appointment with Destiny" by Dr. Grant Jeffrey; Published by WaterBrook Press (Originally published by Frontier Research Publications): 1997

6 Definition of Greek word "kairos": Young's Analytical Concordance to the Bible by Robert Young; Hendrickson Publishers, Box 3473 Peabody, MA 0961–3473 USA (Not dated)

Lightning Source UK Ltd.
Milton Keynes UK
UKOW02f1844291215

265481UK00002B/515/P